# Hands-On Machine Learning with Microsoft Excel 2019

Build complete data analysis flows, from data collection to visualization

**Julio Cesar Rodriguez Martino**

**BIRMINGHAM - MUMBAI**

# Hands-On Machine Learning with Microsoft Excel 2019

**Commissioning Editor:** Sunith Shetty
**Acquisition Editor:** Shrilekha Inani
**Content Development Editor:** Drashti Panchal
**Technical Editor:** Komal Karne
**Copy Editor:** Safis Editing
**Project Coordinator:** Jagdish Prabhu
**Proofreader:** Safis Editing
**Indexer:** Rekha Nair
**Graphics:** Tom Scaria
**Production Coordinator:** Aparna Bhagat

First published: April 2019

Production reference: 1300419

Published by Packt Publishing Ltd.
Livery Place
35 Livery Street
Birmingham
B3 2PB, UK.

ISBN 978-1-78934-537-7

www.packtpub.com

*To my wife, Daniela, always supportive of my many ways of doing what I love.*
*To my father, Julio, who showed me that hard work is the only way. In memory of my mother,*
*Carmen, who would have been proud of this book and of all of my achievements. To my*
*children, Kaysa, Mateo, and Victoria, for their unconditional love.*

`mapt.io`

Mapt is an online digital library that gives you full access to over 5,000 books and videos, as well as industry leading tools to help you plan your personal development and advance your career. For more information, please visit our website.

## Why subscribe?

- Spend less time learning and more time coding with practical eBooks and Videos from over 4,000 industry professionals

- Improve your learning with Skill Plans built especially for you

- Get a free eBook or video every month

- Mapt is fully searchable

- Copy and paste, print, and bookmark content

## Packt.com

Did you know that Packt offers eBook versions of every book published, with PDF and ePub files available? You can upgrade to the eBook version at `www.packt.com` and as a print book customer, you are entitled to a discount on the eBook copy. Get in touch with us at `customercare@packtpub.com` for more details.

At `www.packt.com`, you can also read a collection of free technical articles, sign up for a range of free newsletters, and receive exclusive discounts and offers on Packt books and eBooks.

# Contributors

## About the author

**Julio Cesar Rodriguez Martino** is a machine learning (ML) and artificial intelligence (AI) platform architect, focusing on applying the latest techniques and models in these fields to optimize, automate, and improve the work of tax and accounting consultants. The main tool used in this practice is the MS Office platform, which Azure services complement perfectly by adding intelligence to the different tasks.

Julio's background is in experimental physics, where he learned and applied advanced statistical and data analysis methods. He also teaches university courses and provides in-company training on machine learning and analytics, and has a lot of experience leading data science teams.

*I want to thank my wife, Daniela, for her support and patience throughout the writing of this book.*

# About the reviewer

**Shashidhar Soppin** is a senior software architect with more than 18 years' experience in information technology. He has worked on virtualization, storage, the cloud and cloud architecture, OpenStack, machine learning, deep learning, and Docker container technologies. Primarily his focus is on building new approaches and solutions for Enterprise customers. He is avid author of open source technologies (OSFY), a blogger (LinuxTechi), and a holder of patents. He graduated from BIET, Davangere. In his free time, he loves to travel and read books.

# Packt is searching for authors like you

If you're interested in becoming an author for Packt, please visit `authors.packtpub.com` and apply today. We have worked with thousands of developers and tech professionals, just like you, to help them share their insight with the global tech community. You can make a general application, apply for a specific hot topic that we are recruiting an author for, or submit your own idea.

# Table of Contents

# Preface

Intelligent machines have been a dream of humankind for a very long time. Even if we are far from developing artificial general intelligence, we have made large progress in teaching computers to perform difficult tasks, especially those that are repetitive and time-consuming for humans.

Machine learning models can help any business to make sense of the available data, thus optimizing processes, lowering costs, and generally helping the business to plan ahead. Excel users, at all levels of ability, can feel left behind by this wave of innovation. Everybody is talking about R and Python as the only relevant tools for achieving these tasks. The truth is that a large amount of the work needed to develop and use a machine learning model can be done in Excel.

This book starts by giving a general introduction to machine learning, making the relevant concepts clear and understandable. It shows the reader every step of a machine learning project, from data collection and reading from different data sources, to developing the models and visualizing the results. In every chapter, there are several examples and hands-on exercises that show the reader how to combine Excel functions, add-ins, and connections to databases and cloud services to reach our desired goal: building a full data analysis flow. Different machine learning models are demonstrated and tailored to the type of data to be analyzed.

At the end of the book, the reader is presented with some advanced tools, like Azure Cloud and automated machine learning, which simplify the analysis task and represent the future of machine learning.

## Who this book is for

This book is aimed at data analysts using Excel as their everyday tool, who need to go beyond Power Pivot and use add-ins and other advanced tools. Excel experts wanting to expand their knowledge to take advantage of the new connection possibilities between Excel and Azure will also benefit, as will project managers needing to test machine learning models without writing code.

It is generally taken for granted that, in order to do data science, from data cleansing to visualization and machine learning models, you need to be a Python or R programmer. This is not the case nowadays, and the general tendency seems to be heading toward code-free data science. The reader needs to learn that there are other options, avoiding code to take Excel to the next level and use it as a platform for professional data analysis and visualization.

# What this book covers

Chapter 1, *Implementing Machine Learning Algorithms*, covers the basic machine learning algorithms and how to implement them.

Chapter 2, *Hands-On Examples of Machine Learning Models*, adds some examples of algorithms and their use cases.

Chapter 3, *Importing Data into Excel from Different Data Sources*, covers how to read data from different sources into Excel.

Chapter 4, *Data Cleansing and Preliminary Data Analysis*, describes data preprocessing to prepare data for use in machine learning models.

Chapter 5, *Correlations and the Importance of Variables*, covers feature engineering, which involves identifying redundant variables and useful relationships between variables.

Chapter 6, *Data Mining Models in Excel Hands-On Examples*, describes examples of the most frequently used algorithms in solving business problems such as Market Basket Analysis and customer cohort analysis.

Chapter 7, *Implementing Time Series*, covers time series analysis and prediction.

Chapter 8, *Visualizing Data in Diagrams, Histograms, and Maps*, describes the different available diagrams in Excel and what they are used for.

Chapter 9, *Artificial Neural Networks*, covers advances machine learning in the form of artificial neural networks and deep learning.

Chapter 10, *Azure and Excel - Machine Learning in the Cloud*, covers building and using machine learning models in the cloud, connecting them to Excel.

Chapter 11, *The Future of Machine Learning*, covers the automation of data analysis and predictive models.

# To get the most out of this book

You will need working knowledge of Excel, including how to make cell calculations, input basic functions, and make diagrams. For Chapter 10, *Azure and Excel - Machine Learning in the Cloud* you will need a Microsoft account.

# Download the example code files

You can download the example code files for this book from your account at www.packt.com. If you purchased this book elsewhere, you can visit www.packt.com/support and register to have the files emailed directly to you.

You can download the code files by following these steps:

1. Log in or register at www.packt.com.
2. Select the **SUPPORT** tab.
3. Click on **Code Downloads & Errata**.
4. Enter the name of the book in the **Search** box and follow the onscreen instructions.

Once the file is downloaded, please make sure that you unzip or extract the folder using the latest version of:

- WinRAR/7-Zip for Windows
- Zipeg/iZip/UnRarX for Mac
- 7-Zip/PeaZip for Linux

The code bundle for the book is also hosted on GitHub at https://github.com/PacktPublishing/Hands-On-Machine-Learning-with-Microsoft-Excel-2019. In case there's an update to the code, it will be updated on the existing GitHub repository.

We also have other code bundles from our rich catalog of books and videos available at https://github.com/PacktPublishing/. Check them out!

# Download the color images

We also provide a PDF file that has color images of the screenshots/diagrams used in this book. You can download it here:
http://www.packtpub.com/sites/default/files/downloads/9781789345377_ColorImages.pdf.

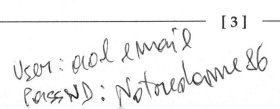

# Conventions used

There are a number of text conventions used throughout this book.

`CodeInText`: Indicates code words in text, database table names, folder names, filenames, file extensions, pathnames, dummy URLs, user input, and Twitter handles. Here is an example: "Navigate to the file's location and open the `homes.csv` file."

**Bold**: Indicates a new term, an important word, or words that you see onscreen. For example, words in menus or dialog boxes appear in the text like this. Here is an example: "Select the full range of cells containing the table, click on **Insert menu**, and select **Charts**."

Warnings or important notes appear like this.

Tips and tricks appear like this.

# Get in touch

Feedback from our readers is always welcome.

**General feedback**: If you have questions about any aspect of this book, mention the book title in the subject of your message and email us at `customercare@packtpub.com`.

**Errata**: Although we have taken every care to ensure the accuracy of our content, mistakes do happen. If you have found a mistake in this book, we would be grateful if you would report this to us. Please visit `www.packt.com/submit-errata`, selecting your book, clicking on the Errata Submission Form link, and entering the details.

**Piracy**: If you come across any illegal copies of our works in any form on the Internet, we would be grateful if you would provide us with the location address or website name. Please contact us at `copyright@packt.com` with a link to the material.

**If you are interested in becoming an author**: If there is a topic that you have expertise in and you are interested in either writing or contributing to a book, please visit `authors.packtpub.com`.

# Reviews

Please leave a review. Once you have read and used this book, why not leave a review on the site that you purchased it from? Potential readers can then see and use your unbiased opinion to make purchase decisions, we at Packt can understand what you think about our products, and our authors can see your feedback on their book. Thank you!

For more information about Packt, please visit `packt.com`.

# Section 1: Machine Learning Basics

The objective of part 1 is to introduce the reader to machine learning and the different types of models used. It will cover supervised and unsupervised learning, the principal division within machine learning. Within these aspects, the difference between regression (continuous target variable) and classification (discrete target variable) will be demonstrated. All points are explained by means of hands-on examples.

This section comprises the following chapters:

- Chapter 1, *Implementing Machine Learning Algorithms*
- Chapter 2, *Hands-On Examples of Machine Learning Models*

# 1
# Implementing Machine Learning Algorithms

Learning has been a matter of study for many years. How human beings acquire new knowledge, from basic survival skills to advanced abstract subjects, is difficult to understand and reproduce in the computer world. Machines learn by comparing examples and by finding similarities in them.

The easiest way for a machine (and also for a human being) to learn is to simplify the problem that needs to be solved. A simplified version of reality, called a model, is useful for this task. Some of the relevant issues to be studied are the minimum number of samples, underfitting and overfitting, relevant features, and how well a model can learn. Different types of target variables require different algorithms.

In this chapter, the following topics will be covered:

- Understanding learning and models
- Focusing on model features
- Studying machine learning models in practice
- Evaluating models

## Technical requirements

There are no technical requirements for this chapter, since it is introductory. The data shown in the sections should be input into an Excel spreadsheet in order to be able to follow the examples.

# Understanding learning and models

The way that humans learn has been studied for many decades now. There are a handful of psychological theories that try to explain how we acquire knowledge, use it, and generalize it in order to apply what we know to completely new scenarios. Taking one step back, we could ask ourselves: what does it mean to learn? We could say that, once we learn something, we are able to repeat it in a more or less detailed way. In reality, learning implies much more than just copying a behavior or memorizing a piece of poetry. In fact, we understand what we learn and are able to generalize that knowledge, which helps us to react correctly to new people, places, and situations.

The need to create a machine that somehow mimics our human behavior and intelligence has been desired for a very long time. Hundreds of years ago, kings were amazed by chess-playing machines, musical instruments that did not require a human player, and mysterious boxes that answered all kinds of questions. These, many times fake, inventions show that one of the greatest dreams of humans is to create an intelligent being, which is able to replicate easy or difficult tasks that are usually performed by people, even when intelligence is an elusive and not easily-defined thing.

Many years have passed, and technology has evolved in such a way that we can now create machines that *think*, or at least seem to. In fact, most of the systems that we call *intelligent* are just able to perform repetitive tasks or react to external inputs according to whatever we have showed them by way of example. As we progress through the chapter, we will see that some of the defined characteristics of human learning and intelligence are already part of modern machine learning systems and some are still the subject of science fiction novels.

By definition, machine learning means to teach a machine or an algorithm to perform tasks. We have been doing this for many years now – it is called **programming**. We give a computer a set of instructions, the order in which they should be executed, and a number of options of how to react to a limited number of inputs. If the input is not known, or if we ask the computer to do something that is not contained in the program, then it will fail, showing an error. The difference between this traditional paradigm and machine learning is that we will never tell the computer exactly what to do. We will either let it discover patterns or show it samples of what we want. We will use programming, of course, but just to define algorithms that *learn* in the sense that was described previously. From finding the straight line that better represents a set of points to driving a car, everything a machine can do is learned in this way.

As babies, we start exploring the world around us. Since we are too young to understand words or examples, we basically experience the world through our senses. We learn the difference between hard and soft, rough and smooth, hot and cold. We can call for attention when we need something, and we can even gain an understanding of the patience levels of our parents and pets. In most cases, nobody sits next to us to explain what we see, hear, feel, taste, and smell. This is an example of what we call *unsupervised learning*.

In unsupervised learning, the training data is "unlabeled". Without our help or intervention, the algorithm/s (or program/s) will find the required connections or unsuspected patterns in the data and learn the details and properties of the dataset.

Later, as we grow up, we understand words and start naming things. Our parents tell us when we see a dog or a cat, we learn our names and theirs, and we learn to identify our toys from among other children's toys (and fight over them). Without even realizing it, we relate some characteristics of objects, animals, and people to their names. These are examples of what is known as *supervised learning*. In the case of a computer, the algorithm is shown as a set of variables that are representative of the properties of the problem and then it learns how these features relate to the name of the label.

Science has shown us the immense complexity of the world that surrounds us. Every branch of scientific knowledge needs advanced mathematical calculations and even completely new ways of looking at data. However, the vast majority of what we can explain is only a fraction of the real world. Whenever we describe a physical phenomenon, an economic or financial event, or try to understand the behavior of individuals and groups, we rely on simplified versions of the real problem. These are called **models** and they make it possible for us to build a mental representation of whatever we are trying to explain. If the model is accurate enough, we will be able to *predict* some future event, or get some approximate value for a certain outcome. As you should have realized by now, this is incredibly powerful. For example, if an artillery soldier is capable of calculating, with accurate precision, where the cannonball is going to hit, then his army has a clear advantage over the enemy in battle. A model is a simplified version of reality that is used to understand a problem and eventually make predictions. Understanding something that your opponent ignores always represents an advantage.

# Learning by example – the linear regression model

Imagine that you and a friend own a small ice cream shop. You are discussing how many **kilograms (kg)** of ice cream to produce each day and you both agree on the fact that the hotter the weather is, the more ice cream will be sold. You add that this is not the only factor to take into account, but there are other variables that can also affect the number of sales. As rational people and good analysts, you decide to run a small experiment by recording the mean temperature during the shop opening hours and the amount of ice cream that is sold. The summer turns out to be particularly rainy, and the temperature variation is high, which helps you to achieve a good range for the variables. The final dataset looks like the following table:

| Mean temperature (°C) | Ice cream sold (kg) |
|---|---|
| 26 | 45 |
| 23 | 42.5 |
| 29 | 53.5 |
| 23 | 35.5 |
| 15 | 32.5 |
| 19 | 34.5 |
| 21 | 33.5 |
| 18 | 35 |
| 15 | 32.5 |
| 25 | 40.5 |
| 25 | 39.5 |
| 16 | 32 |
| 23 | 44.5 |
| 23 | 39.5 |
| 20 | 33 |
| 17 | 26.5 |
| 21 | 37.5 |
| 29 | 49.5 |
| 25 | 40.5 |
| 24 | 44 |

Your model states that the amount of ice cream sold is (directly) proportional to the mean temperature. In order to test this hypothesis, we can make a scatter plot of the collected data:

1. Select the full range of cells containing the table, click on **Insert menu**, and select **Charts**:

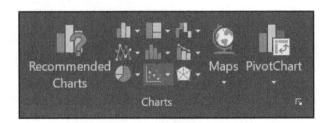

2. Now, click on **Scatter**, as follows:

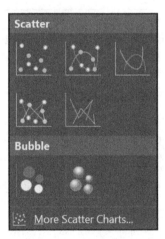

After writing the names of the axis titles, you should get a chart that is similar to the following chart:

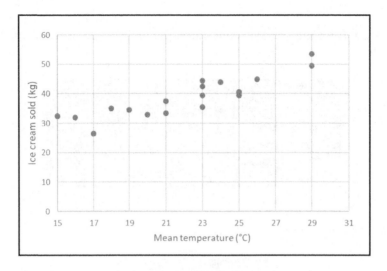

We see that there is indeed a linear correlation and that it is positive (the larger the temperature value, the more ice cream you sell). We can then represent the model using a linear equation, as follows:

$$IC = a * T + b \ (1)$$

Here, *IC* is the amount of ice cream sold, *T* is the mean temperature, and *a* and *b* are constant values to be calculated by a linear regression.

To obtain the values of *a* and *b*, we can use Excel's **Analysis ToolPak** data analysis add-in. If you have not enabled it, refer link `https://support.office.com/en-ie/article/use-the-analysis-toolpak-to-perform-complex-data-analysis-6c67ccf0-f4a9-487c-8dec-bdb5a2cefab6` for instructions on how to do it.

3. Select the data range in your worksheet, go to **Data** in the main menu and then select **Data Analysis**:

4. In the pop-up menu, select **Regression** and click on **OK**:

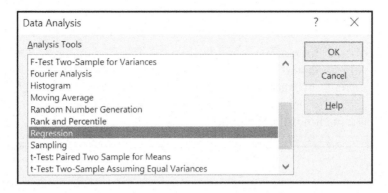

5. Make sure that the $x$ and $y$ ranges are correct ($x$ is temperature and $y$ is ice cream amount). Select **Line Fit Plots** to see the regression line on top of the data points in a new diagram:

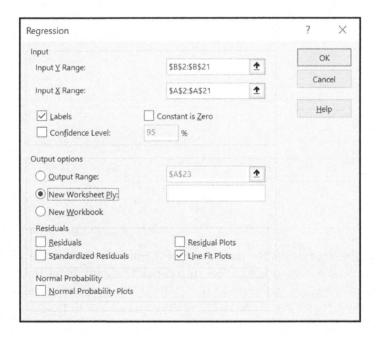

Looking at the output, we see that the line that best fits the data can be written as follows:

$$IC = 1.5 * T + 6 \text{ (2)}$$

There is a standard error for $a$ of $\pm 0.2$, and for $b$ of $\pm 4$. The $R^2$ value is $0.78$, which means that the fit is not very good and only 78% of the variation in ice cream sales can be explained by the mean temperature. So, you and your friend were both right!

The following diagram shows the fitted line:

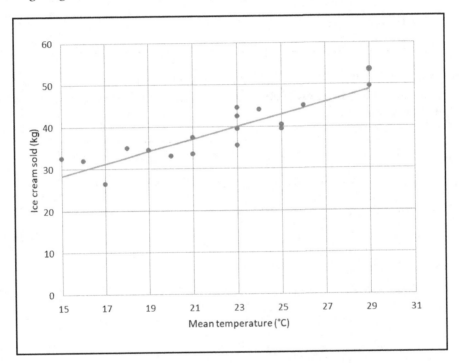

It is clear that the line represents the data quite well, but some points are a little bit off, showing that you need to take other factors into consideration when predicting ice cream consumption. In any case, given the mean forecasted temperature for one day, you can use equation (2) to have a rough estimation of how much ice cream to produce to cover the possible demand.

Keep the rest of the linear regression results to hand, as we are going to use some of them in the following sections.

# Focusing on model features

As a simplified representation of reality, a model also includes a set of variables that contain the relevant information that describes the different parts of the problem we are representing. These variables can be something as concrete as 1 kg of ice cream, as we saw in our previous example, or as abstract as a numerical value that represents how similar the meaning is of two words in a text document.

In the particular case of a machine learning model, these variables are called **features**. Choosing significant features that provide relevant information about the phenomenon that we try to explain or predict is of paramount importance. If we consider unsupervised learning, then the relevant features are those that better represent the clustering or association of information in the dataset. For supervised learning, the most important features are those that highly correlate with the target variable – that is, the value that we want to predict or explain.

The quality of the insights that can be obtained from a machine learning model depends on the features used as input to the model. **Feature selection** and **feature engineering** are regularly-used techniques to improve a model's input. Feature selection is the process of selecting a subset of relevant features for use in any identified model construction. It can also be termed as variable selection or attribute selection. While building any machine learning model, feature selection and data cleaning should be the first and most important steps. Feature engineering is defined as the process of using the domain knowledge of the identified data to create features that make the machine learning algorithm(s) to work. If this is done correctly, then it will increase the predictive power of machine learning algorithms by creating features from new data that is fed into this model or system.

In our previous example, the model features are the mean temperature and the amount of ice cream sold. Since we have already proved that there are more variables involved, we could add some additional features to better explain the daily ice cream consumption. For example, we could take into account which day of the week we are recording data for and include this information as another feature. Additionally, any other relevant information can be represented, more or less accurately, into a feature. In supervised learning, it is customary to call the input variables *features*, and the target or predicted variable *label*.

Features can be numerical (such as the temperature in our previous example), or categorical (such as the day of the week). Since everything in computers is represented as numerical data, categorical data should be converted into numerical form by assigning categories to numbers. One-hot encoding is a process by which categorical variables are converted into a numerical form (or *encoded*) so that they can be input into machine learning algorithms.

Following our example, we could translate the day-of-the-week into day number, as follows:

| Day-of-the-week | Day number |
|---|---|
| Monday | 1 |
| Tuesday | 2 |
| Wednesday | 3 |
| Thursday | 4 |
| Friday | 5 |
| Saturday | 6 |
| Sunday | 7 |

This encoding reflects the order of the days and reserves the highest values for the weekend.

Let's say that you want to be more specific and predict the amount of ice cream for each flavor that you sell. For ease, let's say that you produce four different flavors: chocolate, strawberry, lemon, and vanilla. Could you just assign one number to each flavor, in the same way that you did in the day-of-the-week encoding? The answer, as we shall see, is negative. Let's try it and see what is wrong:

| Flavor | Flavor number |
|---|---|
| Chocolate | 1 |
| Strawberry | 2 |
| Lemon | 3 |
| Vanilla | 4 |

By using this encoding, we are implicitly saying that chocolate is closer to strawberry than to vanilla (1 unit versus 3 units), which is not a real property of the flavors. The right way of translating to numbers is to create binary variables. This approach is known as one-hot encoding and looks like the following table:

| Flavor | Is it chocolate? | Is it strawberry? | Is it lemon? | Is it vanilla? |
|---|---|---|---|---|
| Chocolate | 1 | 0 | 0 | 0 |
| Strawberry | 0 | 1 | 0 | 0 |
| Lemon | 0 | 0 | 1 | 0 |
| Vanilla | 0 | 0 | 0 | 1 |

This method creates some overhead, since it increases the number of features by creating one binary variable for each possible value of the original variable. On the positive side, it correctly calculates the properties of the feature. We will see some examples of this in the next chapter.

Depending on the type of target variable, we can classify them into *regression models* (that is, continuous target variables) or *classification models* (that is, discrete target variables). For example, if we want to predict a real number or an integer number, we use regression, whereas if we are trying to predict a tag with a finite number of options, we use classification.

# Studying machine learning models in practice

We have already seen a very simple example and used it to explain some basic concepts. In the next chapter, we are going to explore more complex models. We restricted ourselves to a very small dataset, just for clarity and to start our journey towards mastering machine learning with an easy task. There are some general considerations that we need to be aware of when working with machine learning models to solve real problems:

- The amount of data is usually very large. In fact, a larger dataset helps to get a more accurate model and a more reliable prediction. Extremely large datasets, usually called *big data,* can present storage and manipulation challenges.
- Data is never clean and ready to use, so data cleansing is extremely important and takes a lot of time.
- The number of features required to correctly represent a real-life problem is often large. The feature engineering techniques previously mentioned are impossible to perform by hand, so automatic methods must be devised and applied.
- It is far more important to assess the predictive power of a combination of input features than the significance of each individual one. Some simple examples of how to select features are given in Chapter 5, *Correlations and the Importance of Variables*.
- It is very unlikely that we will get a very good result with the first model that we apply. Testing and evaluating many different machine learning models implies repeating the same steps several times and usually requires automation as well.

- The dataset should be large enough to use a percentage of the data for training purposes (usually 80%) and the rest for testing. Evaluating the accuracy of a model only on the training data is misleading. A model can be very precise at explaining and predicting the training dataset, but it can fail to generalize and deliver wrong results when presented with new, previously unseen data values.
- Training and test data should be selected, usually at random, from the same full dataset. Trying to make a prediction based on input that lies far away from the training range is unlikely to give good results.

Supervised machine learning models are usually trained using a fraction of the input data and tested on the remaining part. The model can be then used to predict the outcome when fed with new and unknown feature values, as shown in the following diagram:

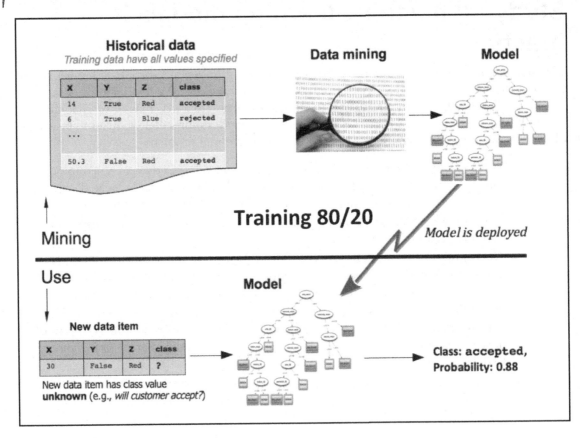

A typical supervised machine learning project includes the following steps:

1. Obtaining the data and merging different data sources (there is more on this in Chapter 3, *Importing Data into Excel from Different Data Sources*)
2. Cleansing the data (you can refer to Chapter 4, *Data Cleansing and Preliminary Data Analysis*)
3. Preliminary analysis and feature engineering (you can refer to Chapter 5, *Correlations and the Importance of Variables*)
4. Trying different models and parameters for each of them, and training them by using a percentage of the full dataset and using the rest for testing
5. Deploying the model so that it can be used in a continuous analysis flow and not only in small, isolated tests
6. Predicting values for new input data

This procedure will become clear in the examples shown in the next chapter.

# Comparing underfitting and overfitting

In the preceding list, step 4 implies an iterative process where we try models, parameters, and features until we get the best result that we can. Let's now think about a classification problem, where we want to separate squares from circles, as shown in the following diagram. At the beginning of the process, we will probably be in a situation that is similar to the first chart (on the left-hand side). The model fails to efficiently separate the two shapes and both sides are a mixture of both squares and circles. This is called **underfitting** and refers to a model that fails to represent the characteristics of the dataset:

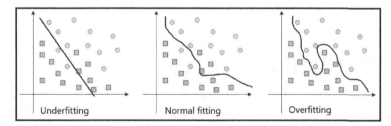

As we continue tuning parameters and adjusting the model to the training dataset, we might find ourselves in a situation that is similar to the third chart (on the right-hand side). The model accurately splits the dataset, leaving only one shape on each side of the border line. Even if this seems correct, it completely lacks generalization. The result adjusts so well to the training data that it will be completely wrong to we test it against a different dataset. This problem is called **overfitting**.

To solve the problem of overfitting in our model, we need to increase its adaptability. However, making it too flexible can also make it bad at predicting. To avoid this, the usual solution is to use *regularization* techniques. There are many similar techniques that can be found in specialized literature, but they are beyond the scope of this book.

The center chart shows a more flexible model; it represents the dataset, but is general enough to deal with new, previously unseen data. It is often time-consuming and it can be difficult to get the right balance in order to build a good machine learning model.

# Evaluating models

Whenever we obtain a result, it is is only as accurate as the model that represents the real problem. It is, therefore, extremely important to understand which methods can be used to evaluate the performance of our models.

When dealing with *classification models* we can use the following methods.

## Analyzing classification accuracy

This is the ratio of the number of **correct predictions (CP)** to the total number of samples:

$$Accuracy = \frac{CP}{TP}$$

Here, *CP* is the number of accurate or correct predictions, and *TP* is the total count of all the predictions that have been made.

## Building the confusion matrix

Let's now think about a binary classification problem. We have a set of samples belonging to two classes: *YES* or *NO*. We can build a machine learning model that outputs a class for each input set of variables. By testing our model on 200 samples, we will get the following results:

| N=200 | Predicted NO | Predicted YES |
|:---:|:---:|:---:|
| **Actual NO** | 60 | 15 |
| **Actual YES** | 25 | 100 |

There are four elements to the confusion matrix:

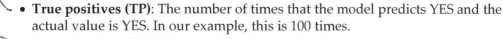

- **True positives (TP)**: The number of times that the model predicts YES and the actual value is YES. In our example, this is 100 times.
- **True negatives (TN)**: The number of times that the model predicts NO and the actual value is NO. In our example, this is 60 times.
- **False positives (FP)**: The number of times that the model predicts YES and the actual value is NO. In our example, this is 15 times.
- **False negatives (FN)**: The number of times that the model predicts NO and the actual value is YES. In this example, this is 25 times.

Then, we calculate the confusion matrix in the following equation:

$$Accuracy = \frac{TP + TN}{N} = \frac{100 + 60}{200} = 0.8$$

# Calculating the Area Under Curve (AUC)

The AUC of a classification model is defined as the probability that the model will rank a random positive example above a random negative example.

Using the confusion matrix, we can define other quantities as follows:

$$TruePositiveRate = \frac{TP}{TP + FN}$$

The **True Positive Rate (TPR) or sensitivity** is the the ratio of data points correctly predicted as positive, with respect to all the data points that have a true value of *YES*:

$$FalsePositiveRate = \frac{FP}{FP + TN}$$

The **False Positive Rate (FPR)** or specificity is the ratio of *NO* data points incorrectly predicted as *YES*, with respect to all *NO* data points.

Both quantities have values in the [0, 1] range. FPR and TPR are both computed at different threshold values and a graph is constructed. The curve is known as **Receiving Operating Characteristic (ROC)**; AUC is the area under that curve, as shown in the following figure:

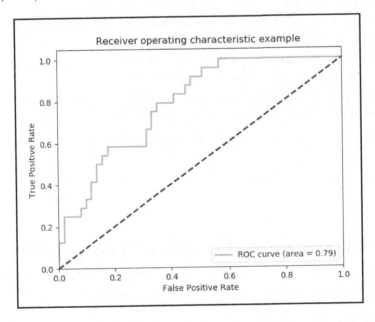

If we instead want to evaluate regression models, we can use the following techniques.

# Calculating the Mean Absolute Error (MAE)

MAE is the mean value of the absolute difference between the real values ($y_j$) and the predicted values ($\hat{y}_j$). It cannot tell us the direction of the error, meaning that the prediction could be above or below the true value. If we have a total of $N$ data points, we can calculate MAE as follows:

$$Mean\,Absolute\,Error = \frac{1}{N}\sum_{1}^{N}|y_j - \hat{y}_j|$$

# Calculating the Mean Squared Error (MSE)

MSE takes the average of the square of the difference between the actual values and predicted values:

$$MeanSquaredError = \frac{1}{N}\sum_{1}^{N}(y_j - \hat{y}_j)^2$$ ✓

No matter what evaluation method we choose, it is extremely important to take into account the business part of the problem. The optimal solution is not always to have the most accurate model, but the one that better satisfies your business needs. It may be the case that a not-so-accurate model that can be built quickly is better than a perfect one that takes a year to produce. Taking into account the dataset imbalance and business needs is important for fine-tuning the model in order to improve the confusion matrix values:

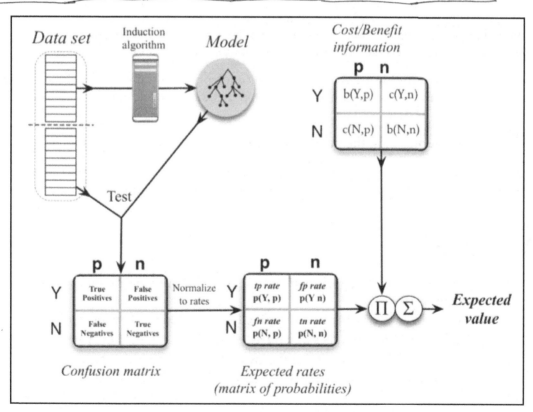

Another important factor to consider is whether we have, in the case of a classification problem, a balanced dataset. A dominant class will lead to a model that mostly predicts the same result every time. For example, a dataset with 99% *YES* labels will produce a machine learning model after training that predicts *YES* for 99% of the input (and it will be right!). There are many known techniques used to balance a dataset and find the problems in our data.

# Summary

In this chapter, we briefly discussed the learning process for machines, which, to some extent, mimics that of human beings. We described how a model, which is a simplified representation of the problem that we want to solve, can be used to apply machine learning to find a solution.

Using a linear regression model, we built a simple supervised predictive model and explained how to use it. We then discussed the difference between regression and classification, and showed the properties of the input variables and features.

Underfitting and overfitting are two of the main concerns when training a machine learning model. We explained what they are and suggested methods to avoid them.

Finally, different types of target variables require different algorithms and evaluation methods to test the quality of the model – we discussed this in detail in the final sections.

In the next chapter, we are going to solve some real-life problems using machine learning and explore how some supervised and unsupervised models are built.

# Questions

1. What is the main difference between classical computer programming and machine learning?
2. How are models classified, considering the type of target variable?
3. What are the different types of models, depending on how they learn?
4. What are the main steps when creating and using a machine learning model?
5. The output of the regression performed in Excel contains information about the residuals. What are they and how are they related to the MAE and MSE?
6. Explain underfitting and overfitting.
7. How can categorical features be used to feed machine learning models?

# Further reading

- *Machine Learning For Beginners*: https://towardsdatascience.com/machine-learning-for-beginners-d247a9420dab
- *Machine Learning basics —It's your cup of tea*: https://hackernoon.com/machine-learning-basics-its-your-cup-of-tea-af4baf060ace

# 2
# Hands-On Examples of Machine Learning Models

Supervised learning is the simplest way of teaching a model about how the world looks. Showing how a given combination of input variables leads to a certain output, that is, using labeled data, makes it possible for a computer to predict the output for another similar dataset that it has never seen. Unsupervised learning deals with finding patterns and useful insights into non-labeled data.

We will study different types of machine learning models, trying to understand the details and actually performing the necessary calculations so that the inner workings of these models are clear and reproducible.

In this chapter, the following topics will be covered:

- Understanding supervised learning with multiple linear regression
- Understanding supervised learning with decision trees
- Understanding unsupervised learning with clustering

## Technical requirements

There are no technical requirements for this chapter. We just need to input the values shown in the tables within each section in an Excel sheet in order to follow the explanation closely.

# Understanding supervised learning with multiple linear regression

In the previous chapter, we followed an example of linear regression using two variables. It is interesting to see how we can apply regression to more than two variables (called **multiple linear regression**) and extract useful information from the results.

Suppose that you are asked to test whether there exists a hidden policy of gender discrimination in a company. You could be working for a law firm that is leading a trial against this company, and they need data-based evidence to back up their claim.

You would start by taking a sample of the company's payroll, including several variables that describe each employee and the last salary increase amount. The following screenshot shows a set of values after they've been entered in an Excel worksheet:

| | A | B | C | D | E | F |
|---|---|---|---|---|---|---|
| 1 | ID | Gender | Score | Years in company | Division | Salary Increase |
| 2 | 1 | F | 11 | 9 | Production | 22 |
| 3 | 2 | F | 89 | 1 | Production | 97 |
| 4 | 3 | F | 21 | 4 | Production | 47 |
| 5 | 4 | F | 81 | 1 | Production | 127 |
| 6 | 5 | F | 31 | 4 | Research | 65 |
| 7 | 6 | F | 71 | 1 | Research | 53 |
| 8 | 7 | F | 11 | 4 | Sales | 74 |
| 9 | 8 | F | 16 | 7 | Production | 18 |
| 10 | 9 | M | 20 | 6 | Research | 129 |
| 11 | 10 | M | 79 | 3 | Sales | 475 |
| 12 | 11 | M | 51 | 3 | Research | 342 |
| 13 | 12 | M | 69 | 2 | Sales | 329 |
| 14 | 13 | M | 30 | 7 | Sales | 185 |
| 15 | 14 | M | 71 | 7 | Sales | 332 |
| 16 | 15 | M | 39 | 1 | Sales | 268 |
| 17 | 16 | M | 89 | 6 | Production | 518 |
| 18 | 17 | M | 50 | 8 | Production | 390 |

There are four numerical features in the dataset:

- ID: The employee identification, which is not relevant to our analysis
- Score: The result of the last employee's performance evaluation
- Years in company: Years that the employee has worked in the company
- Salary increase: Amount in dollars of the last salary increase

The remaining two are categorical:

- Gender: Male (M) or Female (F)
- Division: In which part of the company the employee works

Categorical values need to be encoded before being used in a model. The final data table is as follows:

| | ID | Gender | Score | Years in company | IsProduction? | IsResearch? | IsSales? | Salary Increase |
|---|---|---|---|---|---|---|---|---|
| 20 | | | | | | | | |
| 21 | 1 | 1 | 11 | 9 | 1 | 0 | 0 | 22 |
| 22 | 2 | 1 | 89 | 1 | 1 | 0 | 0 | 97 |
| 23 | 3 | 1 | 21 | 4 | 1 | 0 | 0 | 47 |
| 24 | 4 | 1 | 81 | 1 | 1 | 0 | 0 | 127 |
| 25 | 5 | 1 | 31 | 4 | 0 | 1 | 0 | 65 |
| 26 | 6 | 1 | 71 | 1 | 0 | 1 | 0 | 53 |
| 27 | 7 | 1 | 11 | 4 | 0 | 0 | 1 | 74 |
| 28 | 8 | 1 | 16 | 7 | 1 | 0 | 0 | 18 |
| 29 | 9 | 0 | 20 | 6 | 0 | 1 | 0 | 129 |
| 30 | 10 | 0 | 79 | 3 | 0 | 0 | 1 | 475 |
| 31 | 11 | 0 | 51 | 3 | 0 | 1 | 0 | 342 |
| 32 | 12 | 0 | 69 | 2 | 0 | 0 | 1 | 329 |
| 33 | 13 | 0 | 30 | 7 | 0 | 0 | 1 | 185 |
| 34 | 14 | 0 | 71 | 7 | 0 | 0 | 1 | 332 |
| 35 | 15 | 0 | 39 | 1 | 0 | 0 | 1 | 268 |
| 36 | 16 | 0 | 89 | 6 | 1 | 0 | 0 | 518 |
| 37 | 17 | 0 | 50 | 8 | 1 | 0 | 0 | 390 |

The one-hot encoding is easily obtained by applying standard Excel functions. Assuming B2 is the first cell containing the gender classification, we can enter =IF(B2="F";1;0) in cell B21 and copy this value to all cells down to B37.

**TIP**

Depending on which character is defined in the Windows list separator option, you should either use a comma (,) or a semi-colon (;) in formulas.

To encode the employee's division, we use one-hot encoding (refer to Chapter 1, *Implementing Machine Learning Algorithms*, for a detailed explanation) and create three new variables: IsProduction?, IsResearch?, and IsSales?. We can use Excel functions to calculate the encoding if E2 is the first row containing the Division data, then we can use the =IF(E2="Production";1;0), =IF(E2="Research";1;0), and =IF(E2="Sales";1;0) functions in cells E21, F21, and G21, respectively, and then copy them column-wise down to cells E37, F37, and G37.

Before trying to use regression on the full dataset, we can try some feature engineering. Let's see how well we can predict the salary increase based on which Division each employee works. This will give us an idea of how much the Salary Increase target variable correlates with Division (there will be more details about correlations between variables in Chapter 5, *Correlations and the Importance of Variables*).

Let's follow some simple steps to use the built-in regression tool:

1. Navigate to **Data**.
2. Click on **Data Analysis**, as shown in the following screenshot:

3. Select **Regression**, as shown in the following screenshot:

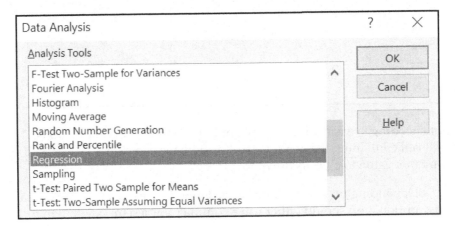

4. As the **Input Y Range**, select the `Salary` data and as the **Input X Range**, select the three `Division` columns:

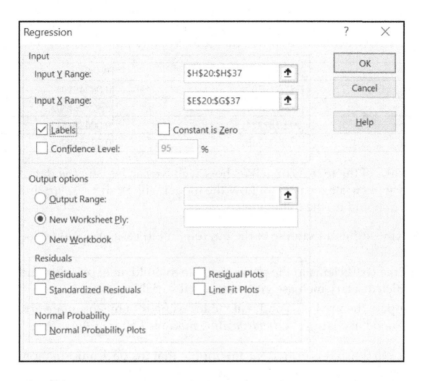

The results show $R^2 = 0.1$, meaning that only 10% of the salary increase is related or can be explained by the fact that the employee belongs to a given division. We can therefore discard these columns as input and concentrate on the rest.

We repeat the regression, now choosing the X values as the columns `Gender`, `Score`, and `Years in company`.

The results are quite different now, with $R^2$ close to 0.85, meaning that 85% of the salary increase values are explained by the chosen variables.

How important is `Gender`? Taking a look at the P-value coefficients that Excel gives us, in the following table, we can see that, according to the P-value associated with the input variables, the most important one is gender, followed by the score and the number of years in the company. It is then clear that gender plays an important role when deciding a salary increase, and we have evidence to prove that the company policy is not gender neutral:

|  | Coefficients | P-value |
|---|---|---|
| **Intercept** | 141.72775 | 0.083481944 |
| **Gender** | -221.9209346 | 6.47796E-05 |
| **Score** | 2.697512241 | 0.004201513 |
| **Years in company** | 8.118352407 | 0.332588988 |

The output results of the regression tell us how well we can explain the data sample, but cannot give us an accurate measure of how the model will predict a salary increase. To explore this, we should do the following:

- Obtain a different sample of the payroll (in our case, we could generate new data by hand)
- Use the coefficients in the previous table to build an expression and calculate the predicted salary increase given the input variables
- Compare the predicted and real values using root mean square error, as explained in `Chapter 1`, *Implementing Machine Learning Algorithms*

Let's see if you can finish this exercise; I am hoping that the basic information that's been provided to you carry this out has been understood.

We have shown how to perform a multiple linear regression in data to extract interesting insights from them. Let's continue with another important machine learning model: decision trees.

# Understanding supervised learning with decision trees

The decision tree algorithm uses a tree-like model of decisions. Its name is derived from the graphical representation of the cascading process that partitions the records. The algorithm chooses the input variables that better split the dataset into subsets that are more pure in terms of the target variable, ideally a subset that contains only one value of this variable. Decision trees are some of the most widely used and easy to understand classification algorithms.

The outcome of the tree algorithm calculation is a set of simple rules that explain which values or intervals of the input values split the original data better. The fact that the results and the path followed to get to them can be clearly shown gives decision trees an advantage over other algorithms. **Explainability** is a serious problem for some machine learning and artificial intelligence systems – which are mostly used as black boxes – and is a study subject in itself.

In complex problems, we need to decide when to stop the tree development. A large number of features can lead to a very large and complex tree, so the number of branches and the length of the tree are usually limited by the user.

Entropy is a very important concept in decision trees and the way of quantifying the purity of each subsample. It measures the amount of information contained in each leaf of the tree. The lower the entropy, the larger the amount of information. Zero entropy means that a subset contains only one value of the target variable, while a value of one represents a subset that contains the same amount of both values. This concept will be explained later with examples.

 Entropy is an indicator of how messy your data is.

Using the entropy that's calculated in every step, the algorithm chooses the best variable to split the data and recursively repeats the same procedure. The user can decide how to stop the calculation, either when all subsets have an entropy of zero, when there are no more features to split by, or a minimum entropy level.

The input features that are best suited for use in a decision tree are the categorical ones. In case of a continuous, numerical variable, it should be first converted into categories by dividing it into ranges; for example, A > 0.5 would be A1 and A ≤ 0.5 would be A2.

Let's look at an example that explains the concept of the decision tree algorithm.

# Deciding whether to train outdoors depending on the weather

Let's suppose we have historical data on the decisions made by an experienced football trainer about training outdoors (outside the gym) or not with her team, including the weather conditions on the days when the decisions were made.

A typical dataset could look as follows:

| | A | B | C | D | E | F |
|---|---|---|---|---|---|---|
| 1 | ID | Temperature | Humidity | Windy | Outlook | Train outside |
| 2 | 1 | Hot | High | False | Rainy | No |
| 3 | 2 | Hot | High | True | Rainy | No |
| 4 | 3 | Hot | High | False | Overcast | Yes |
| 5 | 4 | Mild | High | False | Sunny | Yes |
| 6 | 5 | Cool | Normal | False | Sunny | Yes |
| 7 | 6 | Cool | Normal | True | Sunny | No |
| 8 | 7 | Cool | Normal | True | Overcast | Yes |
| 9 | 8 | Mild | High | False | Rainy | No |
| 10 | 9 | Cool | Normal | False | Rainy | Yes |
| 11 | 10 | Mild | Normal | False | Sunny | Yes |
| 12 | 11 | Mild | Normal | True | Rainy | Yes |
| 13 | 12 | Mild | High | True | Overcast | Yes |
| 14 | 13 | Hot | Normal | False | Overcast | Yes |
| 15 | 14 | Mild | High | True | Sunny | No |
| 16 | | | | | | |

The dataset was specifically created for this example and, of course, might not represent any real decisions.

In this example, the target variable is Train outside and the rest of the variables are the model features.

According to the data table, a possible decision tree would be as follows:

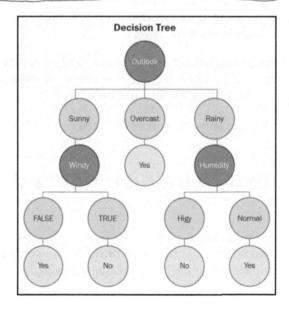

We choose to start splitting the data by the value of the **Outlook** feature. We can see that if the value is **Overcast**, then the decision to train outside is always **Yes** and does not depend on the values of the other features. **Sunny** and **Rainy** can be further split to get an answer.

How can we decide which feature to use first and how to continue? We will use the value of the entropy, measuring how much its value changes when considering different input features.

## Entropy of the target variable

The definition of entropy when looking at a single attribute is as follows:

$$S(f) = \sum_{i=1}^{c} -p_i . log_2(p_i)$$

Here, $c$ is the total number of possible values of the feature $f$, $p_i$ is the probability of each value, and $log_2(p_i)$ is the base two logarithm of the same probability. The calculation details are as follows:

1. We need to count the number of Yes and No decisions in the dataset. In our simple example, they can be counted by hand, but if the dataset is larger, we can use Excel functions:

   *COUNTIF(F2:F15;"Yes")* and *COUNTIF(F2:F15;"No")*

   We then get the calculation that *Yes = 9* and *No = 5*.

2. When applying the entropy formula to the target variable, we get the following:

$$S(Train\ outside) = \sum_{i=1}^{c} -p_i . log_2(p_i) = -9/14 * log2(9/14) - 5/14 * log2(5/14) = 0.94$$

   Here, the probabilities are calculated as the number of *Yes* (9) or *No* (5) over the total number (14).

This calculation can also be easily performed in the Excel sheet using *I3/(I3+J3)\*LOG(I3/(I3+J3);2)-J3/(I3+J3)\*LOG(J3/(I3+J3);2)* with *I3=9* and *J3=5*.

# Entropy of each feature with respect to the target variable

The entropy of two variables $f_1$ and $f_2$ is defined as follows:

$$S(f_1, f_2) = \sum_{v \in f_2} P(v).\, S(v)$$

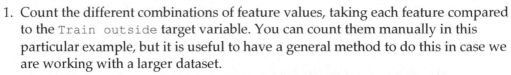

Here, $v$ represents each possible value of $f_2$, $P(v)$ is the probability of each value, and $S(v)$ was defined in the previous equation.

# Frequency table

Let's build a frequency table, which is the usual way of counting the total number of combinations between variables. In our case, we use it to decide which variable choice leads to a larger reduction of the entropy:

1. Count the different combinations of feature values, taking each feature compared to the `Train outside` target variable. You can count them manually in this particular example, but it is useful to have a general method to do this in case we are working with a larger dataset.
2. To count the number of feature combinations, we start by concatenating the values in the data table in pairs. For example, *CONCATENATE(B2;"_";F2)* gives us `Hot_No`.
3. If we copy the formula down to complete the total number of rows, we get all possible combinations of the `Temperature` and `Train outside` variables.
4. If we repeat the same calculation with the rest of the features, the results will be as follows:

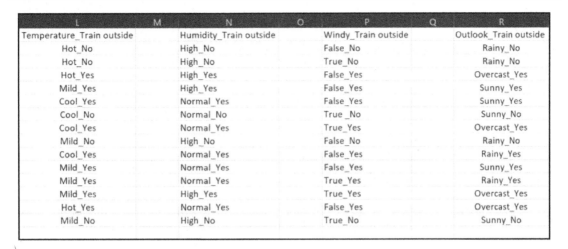

| Temperature_Train outside | Humidity_Train outside | Windy_Train outside | Outlook_Train outside |
|---|---|---|---|
| Hot_No | High_No | False_No | Rainy_No |
| Hot_No | High_No | True_No | Rainy_No |
| Hot_Yes | High_Yes | False_Yes | Overcast_Yes |
| Mild_Yes | High_Yes | False_Yes | Sunny_Yes |
| Cool_Yes | Normal_Yes | False_Yes | Sunny_Yes |
| Cool_No | Normal_No | True_No | Sunny_No |
| Cool_Yes | Normal_Yes | True_Yes | Overcast_Yes |
| Mild_No | High_No | False_No | Rainy_No |
| Cool_Yes | Normal_Yes | False_Yes | Rainy_Yes |
| Mild_Yes | Normal_Yes | False_Yes | Sunny_Yes |
| Mild_Yes | Normal_Yes | True_Yes | Rainy_Yes |
| Mild_Yes | High_Yes | True_Yes | Overcast_Yes |
| Hot_Yes | Normal_Yes | False_Yes | Overcast_Yes |
| Mild_No | High_No | True_No | Sunny_No |

5.  Create pivot tables to count the number of unique values in each column, that is, the number of unique combinations. This can be done by selecting the full range in the column, right-clicking anywhere in the selection, and left-clicking on **Quick Analysis**. The following dialogue will pop up:

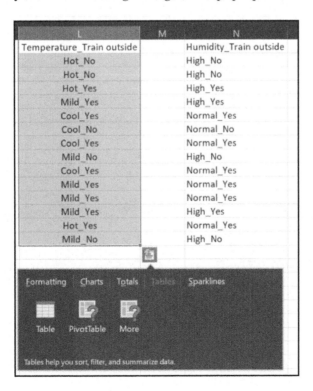

6. Select **Tables** | **PivotTable** to create a table like the following:

| Row Labels | Count of Temperature_Train outside |
|---|---|
| Cool_No | 1 |
| Cool_Yes | 3 |
| Hot_No | 2 |
| Hot_Yes | 2 |
| Mild_No | 2 |
| Mild_Yes | 4 |
| **Grand Total** | **14** |

7. Repeat the same procedure with all columns and build all frequency tables and the two-variable entropy. The resulting tables and the entropy calculations are shown in the following subsection.

# Entropy calculation

The frequency table for the combination Outlook-Train outside is as follows:

| | | Train outside | |
|---|---|---|---|
| | | Yes | No |
| **Outlook** | Sunny | 3 | 2 |
| | Overcast | 4 | 0 |
| | Rainy | 2 | 3 |

Using these values, we get the entropy of two variables, as shown here in detail:

$$S(f_1, f_2) = S(Train\ outside, Outlook) = \sum_{v \in f_2} P(v).\,S(v) =$$

*p(Sunny).S(Sunny)+p(Overcast).S(Overcast)+p(Rainy)\*S(Rainy)=*

*5/14\*(-3/5\*log2(3/5)-2/5\*log2(2/5)) +*

*4/14\*(-4/4\*log2(4/4)-0/4\*log2(0/4))+*

*5/14\*(-2/5\*log2(2/5)-3/5\*log2(3/5))=*

*0.693*

Here, *p(Sunny)* = *(#Yes+#No)/Total entries* = *(2+3)/14*, *p(Overcast)* = *(#Yes+#No)/Total entries* = *(4+0)/14*, and *p(Rainy)* = *(#Yes+#No)/Total entries* = *(2+3)/14*. The entropy values *S(v)* are calculated using the corresponding probabilities, that is, *#Yes* or *#No* over the total *#Yes+#No*.

The frequency table for the combination Temperature-Train outside is as follows:

| | | Train Outside | |
|---|---|---|---|
| | | Yes | No |
| Temperature | Hot | 2 | 2 |
| | Mild | 4 | 2 |
| | Cool | 3 | 1 |

Using these values and an analogous calculation, the entropy is shown in detail here:

$$S(f_1, f_2) = S(Train\ outside, Temperature) = \sum_{v \in f_2} P(v).S(v) =$$

*p(Hot).S(Hot)+p(Mild).S(Mild)+p(Cool)\*S(Cool)=*

$4/14*(-2/4*log_2(2/4)-2/4*log_2(2/4)) +$

$6/14*(-4/6*log_2(4/6)-2/6*log_2(2/6))+$

$4/14*(-3/4*log_2(3/4)-1/4*log_2(1/4)) =$

*0,911*

The frequency table for the combination Humidity-Train outside is as follows:

| | | Train Outside | |
|---|---|---|---|
| | | Yes | No |
| Humidity | High | 3 | 4 |
| | Normal | 6 | 1 |

Using these values, we get the entropy as follows:

$$S(f_1, f_2) = S(Train\ outside, Humidity) = \sum_{v \in f_2} P(v).S(v) =$$

*p(High).S(High)+p(Normal).S(Normal)=*

*7/14\*(-3/7\*log₂(3/7)-4/7\*log₂(4/7)) +*

*7/14\*(-6/7\*log₂(6/7)-1/7\*log₂(1/7))=*

*0,788*

The frequency table for the combination Windy-Train outside is as follows:

| | | Train Outside | |
|---|---|---|---|
| | | Yes | No |
| Windy | TRUE | 6 | 2 |
| | FALSE | 3 | 3 |

Using these values, we get the entropy as follows:

$$S(f_1, f_2) = S(Trainoutside, Windy) = \sum_{v \in f_2} P(v).S(v) =$$

*p(True).S(True)+p(False).S(False)=*

*8/14\*(-6/8\*log₂(6/8)-2/8\*log₂(2/8)) +*

*6/14\*(-3/6\*log₂(3/6)-3/6\*log₂(3/6))*

*=0,892*

# Comparing the entropy differences (information gain)

To know which variable to choose for the first split, we calculate the information gain $G$ when going from the original data to the corresponding subset as the difference between the entropy values:

$$G(f_1, f_2) = S(f_1) - S(f_1, f_2)$$

Here, $S(f_1)$ is the entropy of the target variable and $S(f_1, f2)$ is the entropy of each feature with respect to the target variable. The entropy values were calculated in the previous subsections, so we use them here:

- If we choose *Outlook* as the first variable to split the tree, the information gain is as follows:

  *G(Train outside,Outlook) = S(Train outside) - S(Train outside,Outlook)*
  *= 0.94-0.693=0.247*

- If we choose *Temperature*, the information gain is as follows:

  *G(Train outside,Temperature) = S(Train outside) - S(Train outside,Temperature)*
  *= 0.94-0.911=0.029*

- If we choose *Humidity*, the information gain is as follows:

  *G(Train outside,Humidity) = S(Train outside) - S(Train outside,Humidity)*
  *= 0.94-0.788=0.152*

- Finally, choosing *Windy* gives the following information gain:

  *G(Train outside,Windy) = S(Train outside) - S(Train outside,Windy)*
  *= 0.94-0.892=0.048*

All these calculations are easily performed in a worksheet using Excel formulas.

The variable to choose for the first splitting of the tree is the one showing the largest information gain, that is, *Outlook*. If we do this, we will notice that one of the resulting subsets after the splitting has zero entropy, so we don't need to split it further.

To continue building the tree following a similar procedure, the steps to take are as follows:

1. Calculate *S(Sunny)*, *S(Sunny,Temperature)*, *S(Sunny,Humidity)*, and *S(Sunny,Windy)*.
2. Calculate *G(Sunny,Temperature)*, *G(Sunny,Humidity)*, and *G(Sunny,Windy)*.
3. The larger value will tell us what feature to use to split *Sunny*.
4. Calculate other gains, using *S(Rainy)*, *S(Rainy,Temperature)*, *S(Rainy,Humidity)*, and *S(Rainy,Windy)*.
5. The larger value will tell us what feature to use to split *Rainy*.
6. Continue iterating until there are no features left to use.

As we will see later in this book, trees are never built by hand. It is important to understand how they work and which calculations are involved. Using Excel, it is easy to follow the full process and each step. Following the same principle, we will work through an unsupervised learning example in the next section.

# Understanding unsupervised learning with clustering

Clustering is a statistical method that attempts to group the points in a dataset according to a distance measure, usually the Euclidean distance, which calculates the root of the squared differences between coordinates of a pair of points. To put this simply, those points that are classified within the same cluster are closer (in terms of the distance defined) to each other than they are to the points belonging to other clusters. At the same time, the larger the distance between two clusters, the better we can distinguish them. This is similar to saying that we try to build groups in which members are more alike and are more different to members of other groups.

It is clear that the most important part of a clustering algorithm is to define and calculate the distance between two given points and to iteratively assign the points to the defined clusters, until there is no change in the cluster composition.

There are a few points to consider before trying a clustering analysis. Not every type of data is adequate for clustering. For example, we cannot use binary data since it is not possible to define distances. The values are either 1 or 0, and there is no value in-between. This excludes the type of data generated by one-hot encoding. Only data that shows some ordering or scale is useful for clustering. Even if the data values are real (such as, for example, a client's expenditure amounts or annual income), it is better to group them in a scale of ranges.

Some examples of clustering use cases are as follows:

- Automatic grouping of IT alerts to assign priorities and solve them accordingly
- Analysis of customer communication through different channels (segmentation in time periods)
- Criminal profiling
- Urban mobility analysis
- Fraud detection (looking for outliers)
- Analysis of athletes' performances
- Crime analysis by geography
- Delivery logistics
- Classification of documents

Now, let's go through some examples that explains the concept of clustering algorithms.

# Grouping customers by monthly purchase amount

We will now follow the full calculation and analysis necessary to generate clusters from customer data. This is a simplified version of what would be a typical clustering algorithm, showing all the steps but reducing the number of iterations to make it understandable. Clustering is usually done automatically, but it is important to understand the logic behind the calculation.

The dataset to be used contains the total monthly amount spent by 20 different customers in an online store, corresponding to May, June, and July in a given year. Once typed in an Excel sheet, the data looks like this:

| | A | B | C | D |
|---|---|---|---|---|
| 1 | Customer | May | June | July |
| 2 | 1 | 660.69 | 534.20 | 1867.02 |
| 3 | 2 | 841.70 | 819.17 | 950.46 |
| 4 | 3 | 316.89 | 500.66 | 2056.10 |
| 5 | 4 | 662.35 | 533.69 | 185.63 |
| 6 | 5 | 1372.03 | 2435.76 | 2289.55 |
| 7 | 6 | 4113.02 | 4338.35 | 2868.91 |
| 8 | 7 | 3137.67 | 3436.82 | 3448.07 |
| 9 | 8 | 3587.13 | 2695.09 | 4878.77 |
| 10 | 9 | 4730.14 | 3227.58 | 4232.90 |
| 11 | 10 | 3935.28 | 4404.20 | 4623.66 |
| 12 | 11 | 9946.74 | 9582.46 | 9239.03 |
| 13 | 12 | 9231.08 | 8732.51 | 7782.24 |
| 14 | 13 | 8388.63 | 8314.88 | 8750.93 |
| 15 | 14 | 9377.02 | 8156.16 | 9262.96 |
| 16 | 15 | 8786.33 | 8980.49 | 7708.27 |
| 17 | 16 | 11889.66 | 11902.72 | 11982.64 |
| 18 | 17 | 10000.12 | 10518.74 | 10096.42 |
| 19 | 18 | 11296.65 | 12149.68 | 10423.90 |
| 20 | 19 | 10270.80 | 11107.21 | 10433.03 |
| 21 | 20 | 11100.13 | 12214.41 | 11475.79 |

For each month, we can calculate the main parameters that describe the data: minimum, maximum, median, and average:

| | May | June | July |
|---|---|---|---|
| Minimum | 316.89 | 500.66 | 185.63 |
| Maximum | 11889.66 | 12214.41 | 11982.64 |
| Median | *6559.38* 8388.63 | *6280.18* 8156.16 | *6293.52* 7708.27 |
| Average | 6182.20 | 6229.24 | 6227.81 |

We simply use the Excel built-in functions *MIN()*, *MAX()*, *MEDIAN()*, and *AVERAGE()*, including the full range of each column.

In cluster analysis, it is useful to *normalize* the dataset, that is, to convert all values so that they fall in to the interval [0,1]. This helps us deal with the **outlier** data points, whose value is very different from the majority of points, which can affect the cluster definition. After normalization, those points are not so far away from the rest and can be easily grouped. Clearly, if the goal of the clustering analysis is to find those outliers, it is a better idea to leave the dataset as it is and highlight the difference between the outliers and the rest of the set.

The easiest way to normalize the data is to divide each value by the maximum in the corresponding column. To do this, follow these steps:

1. In cell *G2*, type =B2/$B$24. We are assuming that *B2* is the first value in the May column and that the maximum value is in *B24*.
2. Copy this formula into the whole column. Recall that adding *$* to the cell ID in Excel fixes that value when copying the contents into another cell. The normalized table is then as follows:

| F Customer | G May | H June | I July |
|---|---|---|---|
| 1 | 0.026653 | 0.043736 | 0.15581 |
| 2 | 0.070792 | 0.067066 | 0.079319 |
| 3 | 0.026653 | 0.040989 | 0.17159 |
| 4 | 0.055708 | 0.043694 | 0.015492 |
| 5 | 0.115397 | 0.199417 | 0.191073 |
| 6 | 0.345932 | 0.355183 | 0.239422 |
| 7 | 0.263899 | 0.281374 | 0.287756 |
| 8 | 0.301701 | 0.220648 | 0.407153 |
| 9 | 0.397836 | 0.264244 | 0.353253 |
| 10 | 0.330984 | 0.360574 | 0.385863 |
| 11 | 0.836588 | 0.784521 | 0.771035 |
| 12 | 0.776396 | 0.714935 | 0.649459 |
| 13 | 0.705539 | 0.680743 | 0.730301 |
| 14 | 0.78867 | 0.667749 | 0.773031 |
| 15 | 0.738989 | 0.735237 | 0.643287 |
| 16 | 1 | 0.974481 | 1 |
| 17 | 0.841077 | 0.861175 | 0.842588 |
| 18 | 0.950123 | 0.994701 | 0.869917 |
| 19 | 0.863843 | 0.909353 | 0.870679 |
| 20 | 0.933595 | 1 | 0.957702 |

Let's take a moment to visualize the data and understand it a little more. If we take the columns in pairs, then it is possible to generate scatter plots and try to find clusters visually by following these steps:

1. Select May and June data.
2. Click **Insert | Scatter.**

   The resulting diagram is as follows:

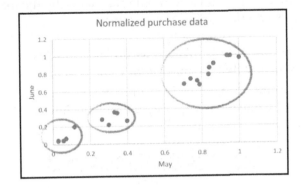

Three clusters can be identified, and are circled in the preceding screenshot. They correspond to groups of customers who spend similar amounts of money monthly.

3. Doing the same with May and July, we get the following diagram:

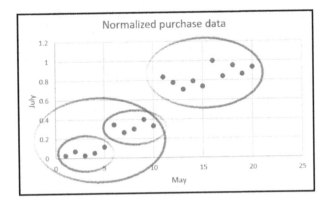

In this case, we could either say that there are two big clusters or that one of them can be further split in two. The separation is not so clear and the choice will depend on other variables (remember that the best model is always the one that best suits the business' needs).

4. Finally, we plot June and July:

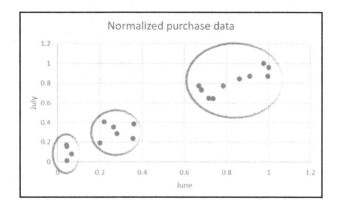

The division of clusters seems even more clear here, and we can circle three sets of points.

What if we want to consider all three months at the same time? There is an iterative process to accomplish this, which is the base of the clustering algorithm known as **K-means**. Let's follow the steps of this algorithm in detail:

1. Decide how many clusters you want to split the data into. This is not an easy decision in general. It will strongly depend on the dataset and, in some cases, will be a matter of testing different values until you get a number of clusters that gives useful insights on the data.
2. Taking into account the previous visual analysis, we decide to choose three as the number of clusters.

3. Take any three points as the center of the clusters. The choice of the starting points is not relevant, as we will repeat the whole process until there is no change in the resulting cluster members. We then choose the first three points in the list, as shown in the following table:

| | May | June | July |
|---|---|---|---|
| Random1 | 0.055568104 | 0.043735522 | 0.15581034 |
| Random2 | 0.07079235 | 0.067065974 | 0.079319396 |
| Random3 | 0.026652635 | 0.040988882 | 0.171590079 |

4. Find the points that are closer to them, computing the distance from all other points to these cluster centers. The Euclidean distance between two points, $P_1 = (x_1, y_1, z_1)$ and $P_2 = (x_2, y_2, z_2)$, is defined as follows:

$$D_E = \sqrt{(x_1 - x_2)^2 + (y_1 - y_2)^2 + (z_1 - z_2)^2}$$

Use Excel's built-in *SUMXMY2([array1];[array2])* function to calculate $(DE)^2$ for each point with respect to the cluster centers.

5. For each data point, you will get three distance values. Pick the smallest one to decide which cluster the point belongs to. For example, for customer ID = 4, we get the following information:

| D1 | D2 | D3 | Cluster |
|---|---|---|---|
| 0.019689391 | 0.004847815 | 0.025218271 | 2 |

Here, *D1, D1,* and *D3* are the distances from the point to the respective cluster centers. The smallest distance tells us that this point belongs to cluster two. As an example, *D1* for customer ID = 4 is calculated as =*SUMXMY2(B5:D5;$B$23:$D$23)*, assuming that **Random1** May and **Random1** June are in cells *$B$23* and *$D$23*, respectively.

6. The complete resulting data table is as follows:

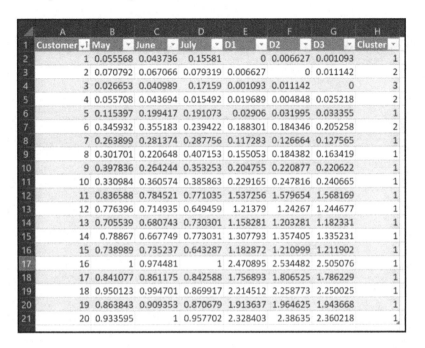

| | A | B | C | D | E | F | G | H |
|---|---|---|---|---|---|---|---|---|
| 1 | Customer | May | June | July | D1 | D2 | D3 | Cluster |
| 2 | 1 | 0.055568 | 0.043736 | 0.15581 | 0 | 0.006627 | 0.001093 | 1 |
| 3 | 2 | 0.070792 | 0.067066 | 0.079319 | 0.006627 | 0 | 0.011142 | 2 |
| 4 | 3 | 0.026653 | 0.040989 | 0.17159 | 0.001093 | 0.011142 | 0 | 3 |
| 5 | 4 | 0.055708 | 0.043694 | 0.015492 | 0.019689 | 0.004848 | 0.025218 | 2 |
| 6 | 5 | 0.115397 | 0.199417 | 0.191073 | 0.02906 | 0.031995 | 0.033355 | 1 |
| 7 | 6 | 0.345932 | 0.355183 | 0.239422 | 0.188301 | 0.184346 | 0.205258 | 2 |
| 8 | 7 | 0.263899 | 0.281374 | 0.287756 | 0.117283 | 0.126664 | 0.127565 | 1 |
| 9 | 8 | 0.301701 | 0.220648 | 0.407153 | 0.155053 | 0.184382 | 0.163419 | 1 |
| 10 | 9 | 0.397836 | 0.264244 | 0.353253 | 0.204755 | 0.220877 | 0.220622 | 1 |
| 11 | 10 | 0.330984 | 0.360574 | 0.385863 | 0.229165 | 0.247816 | 0.240665 | 1 |
| 12 | 11 | 0.836588 | 0.784521 | 0.771035 | 1.537256 | 1.579654 | 1.568169 | 1 |
| 13 | 12 | 0.776396 | 0.714935 | 0.649459 | 1.21379 | 1.24267 | 1.244677 | 1 |
| 14 | 13 | 0.705539 | 0.680743 | 0.730301 | 1.158281 | 1.203281 | 1.182331 | 1 |
| 15 | 14 | 0.78867 | 0.667749 | 0.773031 | 1.307793 | 1.357405 | 1.335231 | 1 |
| 16 | 15 | 0.738989 | 0.735237 | 0.643287 | 1.182872 | 1.210999 | 1.211902 | 1 |
| 17 | 16 | 1 | 0.974481 | 1 | 2.470895 | 2.534482 | 2.505076 | 1 |
| 18 | 17 | 0.841077 | 0.861175 | 0.842588 | 1.756893 | 1.806525 | 1.786229 | 1 |
| 19 | 18 | 0.950123 | 0.994701 | 0.869917 | 2.214512 | 2.258773 | 2.250025 | 1 |
| 20 | 19 | 0.863843 | 0.909353 | 0.870679 | 1.913637 | 1.964625 | 1.943668 | 1 |
| 21 | 20 | 0.933595 | 1 | 0.957702 | 2.328403 | 2.38635 | 2.360218 | 1 |

**TIP**

The last column can be created by typing the following formula into the first row and then copying it down: *=IF(E2=MIN(E2:G2);1;IF(F2=MIN(E2:G2);2;3))*.

According to the table, our first result is really unbalanced. Most of the points fall in cluster one, a few in cluster two, and only one in cluster three. We need to continue the calculations and see how the result evolves. Follow these steps:

1. Instead of choosing random points, we will now use the mean values of the clusters we obtained.

2. Order the table by cluster number. The resulting table is a little different now, as follows:

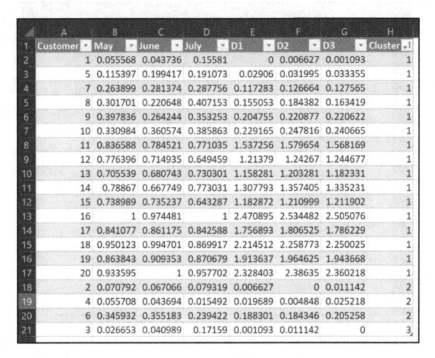

| | A | B | C | D | E | F | G | H |
|---|---|---|---|---|---|---|---|---|
| 1 | Customer | May | June | July | D1 | D2 | D3 | Cluster |
| 2 | 1 | 0.055568 | 0.043736 | 0.15581 | 0 | 0.006627 | 0.001093 | 1 |
| 3 | 5 | 0.115397 | 0.199417 | 0.191073 | 0.02906 | 0.031995 | 0.033355 | 1 |
| 4 | 7 | 0.263899 | 0.281374 | 0.287756 | 0.117283 | 0.126664 | 0.127565 | 1 |
| 5 | 8 | 0.301701 | 0.220648 | 0.407153 | 0.155053 | 0.184382 | 0.163419 | 1 |
| 6 | 9 | 0.397836 | 0.264244 | 0.353253 | 0.204755 | 0.220877 | 0.220622 | 1 |
| 7 | 10 | 0.330984 | 0.360574 | 0.385863 | 0.229165 | 0.247816 | 0.240665 | 1 |
| 8 | 11 | 0.836588 | 0.784521 | 0.771035 | 1.537256 | 1.579654 | 1.568169 | 1 |
| 9 | 12 | 0.776396 | 0.714935 | 0.649459 | 1.21379 | 1.24267 | 1.244677 | 1 |
| 10 | 13 | 0.705539 | 0.680743 | 0.730301 | 1.158281 | 1.203281 | 1.182331 | 1 |
| 11 | 14 | 0.78867 | 0.667749 | 0.773031 | 1.307793 | 1.357405 | 1.335231 | 1 |
| 12 | 15 | 0.738989 | 0.735237 | 0.643287 | 1.182872 | 1.210999 | 1.211902 | 1 |
| 13 | 16 | 1 | 0.974481 | 1 | 2.470895 | 2.534482 | 2.505076 | 1 |
| 14 | 17 | 0.841077 | 0.861175 | 0.842588 | 1.756893 | 1.806525 | 1.786229 | 1 |
| 15 | 18 | 0.950123 | 0.994701 | 0.869917 | 2.214512 | 2.258773 | 2.250025 | 1 |
| 16 | 19 | 0.863843 | 0.909353 | 0.870679 | 1.913637 | 1.964625 | 1.943668 | 1 |
| 17 | 20 | 0.933595 | 1 | 0.957702 | 2.328403 | 2.38635 | 2.360218 | 1 |
| 18 | 2 | 0.070792 | 0.067066 | 0.079319 | 0.006627 | 0 | 0.011142 | 2 |
| 19 | 4 | 0.055708 | 0.043694 | 0.015492 | 0.019689 | 0.004848 | 0.025218 | 2 |
| 20 | 6 | 0.345932 | 0.355183 | 0.239422 | 0.188301 | 0.184346 | 0.205258 | 2 |
| 21 | 3 | 0.026653 | 0.040989 | 0.17159 | 0.001093 | 0.011142 | 0 | 3 |

3. Use the *MEAN()* function to calculate the average value per cluster for each month. You should get the same results that are shown in the following table:

| | May | June | July |
|---|---|---|---|
| **Mean1** | 0.618762809 | 0.605805489 | 0.618056642 |
| **Mean2** | 0.157477363 | 0.155314048 | 0.111411008 |
| **Mean3** | 0.026652635 | 0.040988882 | 0.171590079 |

As an example, **Mean1** corresponding to May is calculated as *AVERAGE(B2:B17)*.

4. Using the same formulas as before and calculating the distances from all other points to the mean values, you get a table similar to this:

| Customer | May | June | July | D1 | D2 | D3 | Cluster |
|---|---|---|---|---|---|---|---|
| 1 | 0.055568 | 0.043736 | 0.15581 | 0.846783 | 0.024807 | 0.001093 | 3 |
| 2 | 0.070792 | 0.067066 | 0.079319 | 0.88075 | 0.016332 | 0.011142 | 3 |
| 3 | 0.026653 | 0.040989 | 0.17159 | 0.868945 | 0.033807 | 0 | 3 |
| 4 | 0.055708 | 0.043694 | 0.015492 | 0.996086 | 0.032017 | 0.025218 | 3 |
| 5 | 0.115397 | 0.199417 | 0.191073 | 0.600844 | 0.010062 | 0.033355 | 2 |
| 6 | 0.345932 | 0.355183 | 0.239422 | 0.280613 | 0.091849 | 0.205258 | 2 |
| 7 | 0.263899 | 0.281374 | 0.287756 | 0.340283 | 0.058314 | 0.127565 | 2 |
| 8 | 0.301701 | 0.220648 | 0.407153 | 0.293354 | 0.112533 | 0.163419 | 2 |
| 9 | 0.397836 | 0.264244 | 0.353253 | 0.235594 | 0.128126 | 0.220622 | 2 |
| 10 | 0.330984 | 0.360574 | 0.385863 | 0.196869 | 0.14756 | 0.240665 | 2 |
| 11 | 0.836588 | 0.784521 | 0.771035 | 0.102789 | 1.292196 | 1.568169 | 1 |
| 12 | 0.776396 | 0.714935 | 0.649459 | 0.037743 | 0.985731 | 1.244677 | 1 |
| 13 | 0.705539 | 0.680743 | 0.730301 | 0.025745 | 0.959473 | 1.182331 | 1 |
| 14 | 0.78867 | 0.667749 | 0.773031 | 0.056723 | 1.098735 | 1.335231 | 1 |
| 15 | 0.738989 | 0.735237 | 0.643287 | 0.031843 | 0.957358 | 1.211902 | 1 |
| 16 | 1 | 0.974481 | 1 | 0.427144 | 2.17047 | 2.505076 | 1 |
| 17 | 0.841077 | 0.861175 | 0.842588 | 0.165051 | 1.500166 | 1.786229 | 1 |
| 18 | 0.950123 | 0.994701 | 0.869917 | 0.324473 | 1.908189 | 2.250025 | 1 |
| 19 | 0.863843 | 0.909353 | 0.870679 | 0.216023 | 1.644013 | 1.943668 | 1 |
| 20 | 0.933595 | 1 | 0.957702 | 0.369867 | 2.032061 | 2.360218 | 1 |

After the second iteration, a few more points, which, when moved away from cluster one, now belong to cluster two and three.

5. Repeat the calculation one more time. The new mean values, according to the preceding table, are as follows:

| | May | June | July |
|---|---|---|---|
| Mean1 | 0.843481911 | 0.832289469 | 0.810799822 |
| Mean2 | 0.292624962 | 0.280240044 | 0.310753303 |
| Mean3 | 0.052180197 | 0.048870976 | 0.105552835 |

6. The table containing the distances and cluster numbers can be given as follows:

| Customer | May | June | July | D1 | D2 | D3 | Cluster |
|---|---|---|---|---|---|---|---|
| 1 | 0.055568 | 0.043736 | 0.15581 | 1.671637 | 0.136138 | 0.002564 | 3 |
| 2 | 0.070792 | 0.067066 | 0.079319 | 1.71768 | 0.148215 | 0.001366 | 3 |
| 3 | 0.026653 | 0.040989 | 0.17159 | 1.701956 | 0.147349 | 0.005075 | 3 |
| 4 | 0.055708 | 0.043694 | 0.015492 | 1.874987 | 0.199264 | 0.00815 | 3 |
| 5 | 0.115397 | 0.199417 | 0.191073 | 1.314697 | 0.052266 | 0.033974 | 3 |
| 6 | 0.345932 | 0.355183 | 0.239422 | 0.801659 | 0.013546 | 0.198038 | 2 |
| 7 | 0.263899 | 0.281374 | 0.287756 | 0.913 | 0.001355 | 0.13208 | 2 |
| 8 | 0.301701 | 0.220648 | 0.407153 | 0.830561 | 0.012926 | 0.182731 | 2 |
| 9 | 0.397836 | 0.264244 | 0.353253 | 0.730625 | 0.013132 | 0.227219 | 2 |
| 10 | 0.330984 | 0.360574 | 0.385863 | 0.66574 | 0.013567 | 0.253464 | 2 |
| 11 | 0.836588 | 0.784521 | 0.771035 | 0.003911 | 0.762054 | 1.599342 | 1 |
| 12 | 0.776396 | 0.714935 | 0.649459 | 0.044303 | 0.537715 | 1.263963 | 1 |
| 13 | 0.705539 | 0.680743 | 0.730301 | 0.048474 | 0.506921 | 1.216451 | 1 |
| 14 | 0.78867 | 0.667749 | 0.773031 | 0.031504 | 0.609925 | 1.370955 | 1 |
| 15 | 0.738989 | 0.735237 | 0.643287 | 0.048399 | 0.516842 | 1.231963 | 1 |
| 16 | 1 | 0.974481 | 1 | 0.080513 | 1.457411 | 2.555153 | 1 |
| 17 | 0.841077 | 0.861175 | 0.842588 | 0.001851 | 0.921132 | 1.825415 | 1 |
| 18 | 0.950123 | 0.994701 | 0.869917 | 0.041245 | 1.255422 | 2.285148 | 1 |
| 19 | 0.863843 | 0.909353 | 0.870679 | 0.009939 | 1.035589 | 1.984642 | 1 |
| 20 | 0.933595 | 1 | 0.957702 | 0.057827 | 1.347439 | 2.407696 | 1 |

After the third iteration, only one point changed cluster, from two to three; so, we are getting close to the final result. You should be able to perform one more iteration, following the same steps, proving that it does not change the clustering labels and meaning that the calculations converged to a stable number of clusters.

Real-life datasets might not converge so fast. What we have shown is a simplified example, good enough to show every step of the iteration, understand them, and get to a reasonable result. Clustering is not usually calculated manually, but performed by pre-built algorithms.

In the following chapter, you will learn how to import data from different sources to Excel, so you don't need to type in the values manually. This will give you a starting point to analyze real data, usually containing many more variables and values than the examples shown in this chapter.

# Summary

In this chapter, we have described real life examples of supervised and unsupervised machine learning models that have been applied to solving problems. We covered multiple regression, decision trees, and clustering. We have also shown how to choose and transform the input variables or features to be ingested by the models.

This chapter only shows the basic principles of each algorithm. In real data analysis and prediction using machine learning, models are already programmed and can be used as black boxes. It is, therefore, extremely important to understand the basics of each model and know whether we are using it correctly.

In the following chapters, we will focus on how to extract the data from different sources, transform it according to our needs, and use previously built models for analysis.

# Questions

1. Why is it important to encode categorical features?
2. What are the different ways to stop a decision tree calculation?
3. `Temperature_hot` has an entropy value of one in the example. Why?
4. Following the diagram of the decision tree at the beginning of the *Understanding supervised learning with decision trees* section, what would be the path to decide whether or not to train outside? Consider using `IF` statements.
5. Would the cluster distribution change if we choose different starting points? You can read about this in the recommended articles.
6. Is the clustering that's obtained with iterative analysis the same as the one that's determined visually? Why?

# Further reading

- *How to Interpret Regression Analysis Results: P-values and Coefficients*: http://blog.minitab.com/blog/adventures-in-statistics-2/how-to-interpret-regression-analysis-results-p-values-and-coefficients
- *Teaching Decision Tree Classification Using Microsoft Excel INFORMS Transactions on Education* 11(3), pp. 123–131, by Kaan Ataman, George Kulick, Thaddeus Sim: https://pubsonline.informs.org/doi/10.1287/ited.1100.0060
- *A Review of K-mean Algorithm*, International Journal of Engineering Trends and Technology (IJETT) – Volume 4 Issue 7- July 2013: http://www.ijettjournal.org/volume-4/issue-7/IJETT-V4I7P139.pdf

# Section 2: Data Collection and Preparation 2

Once this is complete, the reader should have a very clear understanding of how to collect and cleanse data, recognizing that there are different data sources, formats, and volumes. It will also be clear that it is necessary to understand the data and the problem before applying any machine learning model.

This section comprises the following chapters:

- Chapter 3, *Importing Data into Excel from Different Data Sources*
- Chapter 4, *Data Cleansing and Preliminary Data Analysis*
- Chapter 5, *Correlations and the Importance of Variables*

# 3
# Importing Data into Excel from Different Data Sources

Serious data analysis and machine learning cannot be done by using hand-typed data. Data sources come in different flavors and sizes, and Excel can handle many of them. This chapter deals with how to import data from different sources, which is the first step of any analysis.

Get & Transform (known as **Power Query** in Excel versions before 2016) is a powerful tool that you can use to load data from different sources and transform it. These transformations are necessary so that you have a clean data sample that you can then use to train and test any machine learning model.

If you are running Excel 2010 SP1 or Excel 2013, you need to download and install Power Query. Refer link `https://www.microsoft.com/en-us/download/details.aspx?id=39379` for instructions on how to install it.

In this chapter, we will cover the following topics:

- Importing data from a text file
- Importing data from another Excel workbook
- Importing data from a web page
- Importing data from Facebook
- Importing data from a JSON file
- Importing data from a database

# Technical requirements

You will need to download the `homes.csv`, `homes.txt`, `titanic.xls`, and `azure_text_analytics.json` files from this book's GitHub repository at `https://github.com/PacktPublishing/Hands-On-Machine-Learning-with-Microsoft-Excel-2019/tree/master/Chapter03`.

# Importing data from a text file

The more commonly used data text file is **comma-separated values (CSV)**. As the name suggests, values are written to the file in rows and, for each row, a comma separates the values belonging to each column. Open a new workbook and follow these steps:

1. Click on **Data.**
2. Navigate to **Get Data** | **From File** | **From Text/CSV**:

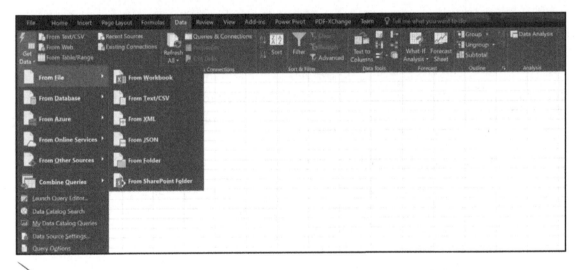

3. Navigate to the file's location and open the `homes.csv` file.

4. A window will pop up, showing you a preview of the file's contents, as shown in the following screenshot:

We can see that Excel correctly identifies the different columns by using the right delimiter (comma). It also tries to detect the data types automatically. There is a small problem, though. This file is not pure CSV, and has an extra line at the beginning, showing us where it was downloaded from originally. This is good for giving credit to the original author, but it confuses the loading process a bit. Fortunately, this situation has already been taken into account. To solve this issue, click on **Edit**.

on Transform Data

5. A window will pop up, containing many options to deal with these file format differences:

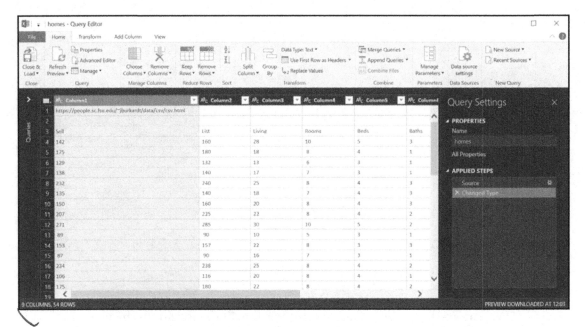

6. Navigate to **Remove Rows** | **Remove Top Rows.**
7. You will see the option to specify how many rows you want to skip. In this file, we need to skip 2 rows, as shown in the following screenshot:

After removing the rows, we keep only the data of interest. You will notice that the file headers haven't been used as column names yet, which would be ideal. To correct this, click on **Use First Row as Headers**.

8. The result of this is shown in the following screenshot:

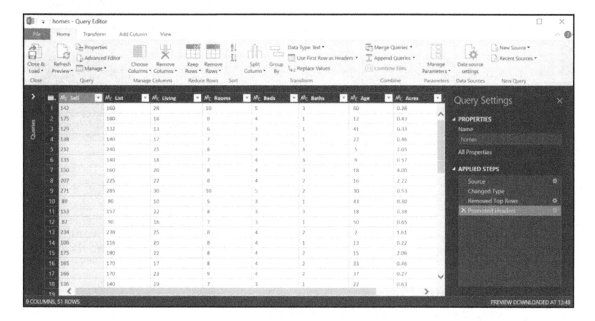

Note that a list of the steps have been applied to the input data, to the right of the table. This allows you to undo any of your actions and is useful to keep track of what you have done, especially if you make more complicated transformations, like the ones we will show you in the next chapter.

The process is almost ready, except for the data type of each column. Originally, it was set automatically to text, since the first two rows, that we skipped later, were evaluated as not containing numerical data. There are two types of columns: Acres shows decimal numbers, while the rest show integer or whole numbers. To define the data type correctly, perform the following steps:

1. Select Acres.
2. Navigate to **Data Type** in the **Transform** menu.
3. Change the type to **Decimal Number.**
4. Select the rest of the columns and change the type to **Whole Number** to fix the other columns.

5. Finally, click on **Close & Load**. You will see the following data table:

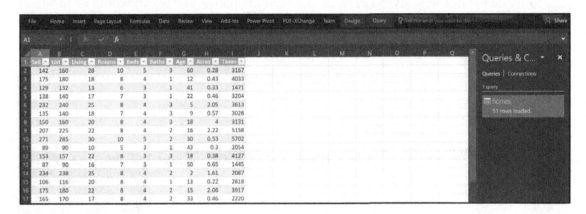

This table looks like any Excel table, except that we can always double-click on the query (called `homes`) and perform more transformations or even undo the ones we've already made.

If the file is not a CSV file but just a text file that's using a different separator, we can still load it using a similar procedure. We just repeat the steps we used for importing the CSV file:

1. Click on **Data**.
2. Navigate to **Get Data | From File | From Text/CSV**.
3. Navigate to the file's location and open `homes.txt`. You will see the following preview:

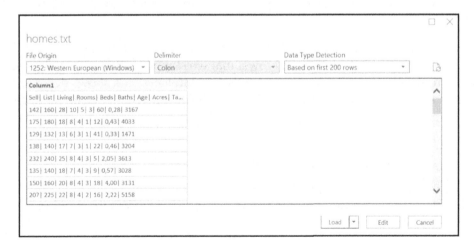

In this case, there are no extra lines at the beginning, but we can see that Excel fails to identify the column delimiter, which is the | character. To fix this, select **Custom** from the drop-down menu.

4. Type |.
5. The result is that the data is now correctly separated into columns. The columns are automatically labeled using the file header and the data types are guessed correctly, as shown in the following screenshot:

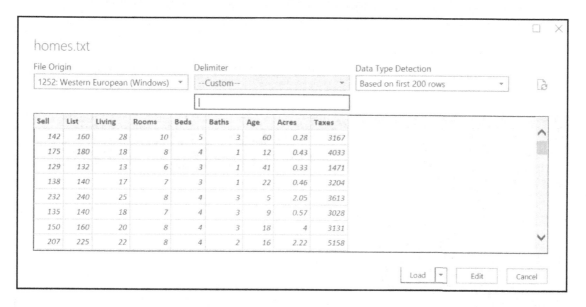

The final result is a table that is identical to the one we loaded from homes.csv, but that took less steps to obtain since the file structure was simpler.

In this section, we have learned how to import a text file into Excel, which is the simplest case. Let's continue with some more complex examples.

# Importing data from another Excel workbook

Why would we import data from an Excel workbook if we can just open it? The main reason is to take advantage of the transformations we can do using Get & Transform. We will show this by using a file containing real data from the Titanic passengers, which is often used to test machine learning classification models and predict whether a given passenger survived the tragedy or not.

Let's follow some simple steps to load and transform the data. While in a new workbook, follow these steps:

1. Click on **Data.**
2. Navigate to **Get Data | From File | From Workbook**, as shown in the following screenshot:

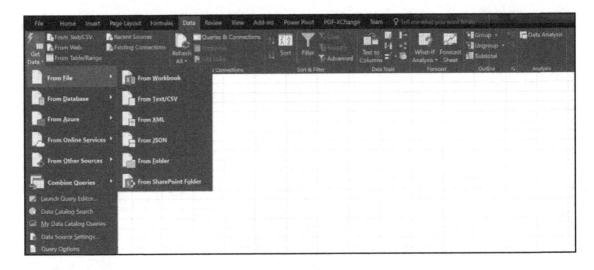

The preview window is slightly different to the one we see when opening a CSV file, as you can see in the following screenshot:

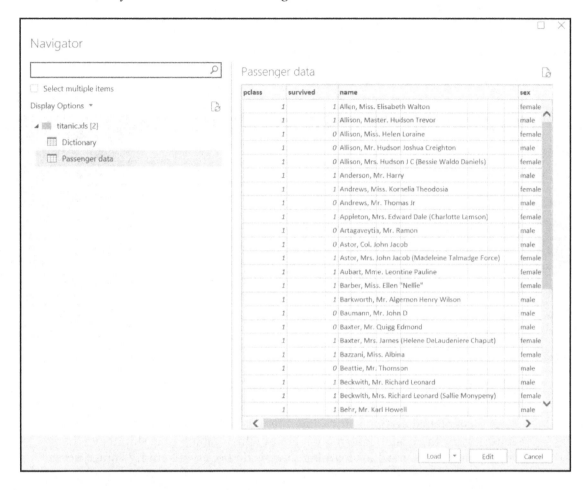

In the left part of the preview, you can see a folder named `titanic.xls`, which represents the file, and below that the worksheets contained within. `Dictionary` is just a short description of the variables; the data is contained in the `Passenger data` sheet.

When this item is selected, we will see a table containing the data. We can click on **Load** and put the data in our worksheet, but first we will try one of the transformations that we will discuss in detail in the next chapter. To do this, click on **Edit** and get to the **Query Editor**, as shown in the following screenshot:

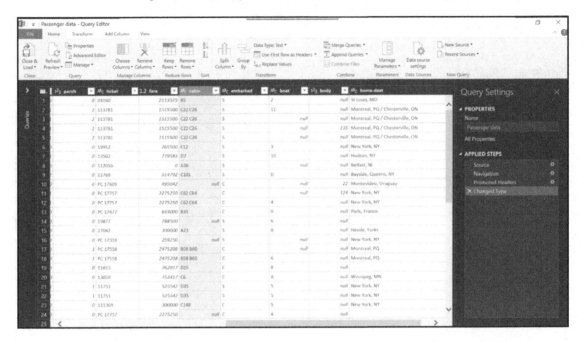

The columns are identified correctly and the names that are taken from the column names are placed in the input file. You can see that one of the columns, cabin, contains missing values, identified as null. This means that, for those passengers, there is no information about which cabin in the ship they where occupying. Some machine learning models do not accept empty values, so we need to fix this by selecting the column, as shown in the preceding screenshot.

3. Click on **Replace Values** in the **Transform** menu.
4. You will get a pop-up dialog where you can tell Excel to replace null with Unknown, as shown in the following screenshot:

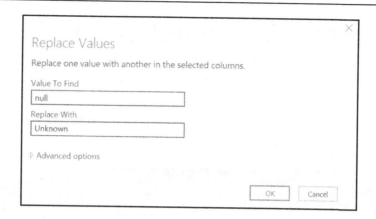

The result is what you can see in the following screenshot, where all `null` values are replaced with `Unknown`. This is both more elegant and easier to manage by machine learning models:

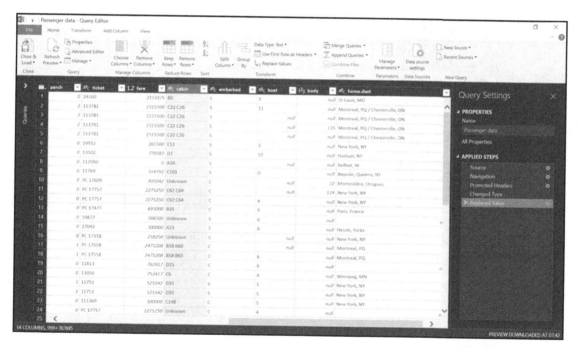

Many different transformations can be performed on the data using the **Query Editor**. We will show other examples in the next chapter. You should try to test different options as well.

# Importing data from a web page

If a web page contains data in tabular form, then Excel is able to import these tables automatically. As an example, we will import a table from the Wikipedia page about Excel. Here's how we will go about it:

1. Click on **Data** and then navigate to **Get Data** I **From Other Sources** I **From Web**, as shown in the following screenshot:

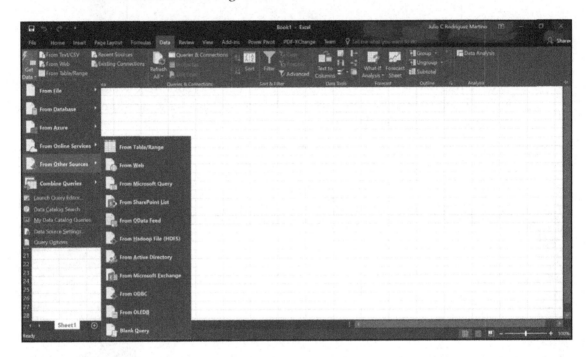

2. In the dialog that pops up, we type in the URL of the mentioned web page and click **OK**, as shown in the following screenshot:

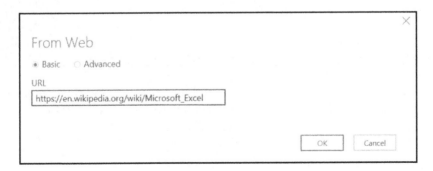

3. Now, we will be able to see a list of available tables. Pick the one showing Excel's release history. A table preview is shown to the right, as shown in the following screenshot:

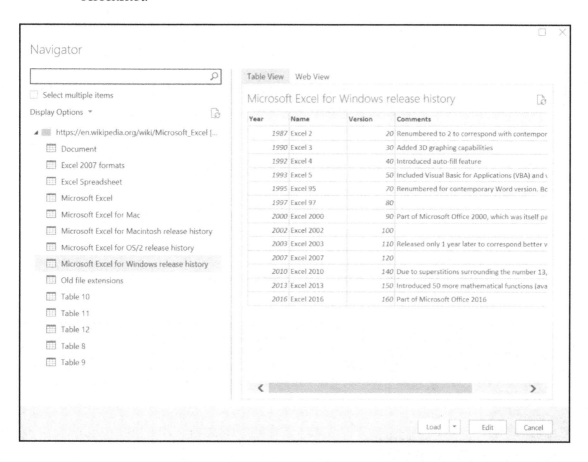

4. As we did before, we can just load the data or edit it, transforming the values according to our needs. The final result is an Excel table.

> We also have the choice of changing to web view and seeing the target web page as we would in Internet Explorer, which can help us to identify which information is useful for our analysis.

We have seen how easy it is to import data from a web page. Now, let's explore importing data from one of the most popular websites: Facebook.

# Importing data from Facebook

It is possible to import data directly from a Facebook profile or page. If we want to, for example, register the dates and times when a new post appears, we could follow these steps:

1. Click on **Data.**
2. Navigate to **Get Data** | **From Online Services** | **From Facebook**, as shown in the following screenshot:

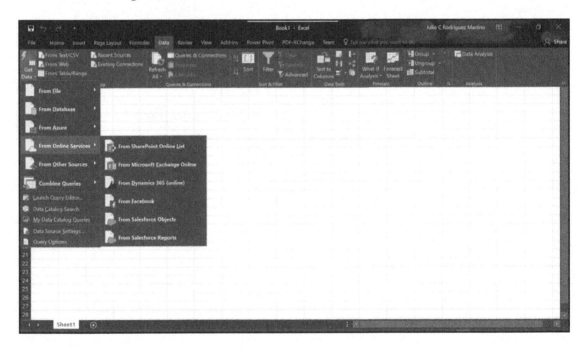

3. You need to specify the user or page name, which is the last part of the page URL. As an example, I will use my own Facebook page, which is the default option. The first time you connect, you will have to log in with your username and password (to connect to Facebook from Excel, you need a Facebook profile). The following dialog will appear:

4. We will choose to get information about **Posts**. After clicking **OK**, we get the following screen (I will only show it partially, to protect my privacy):

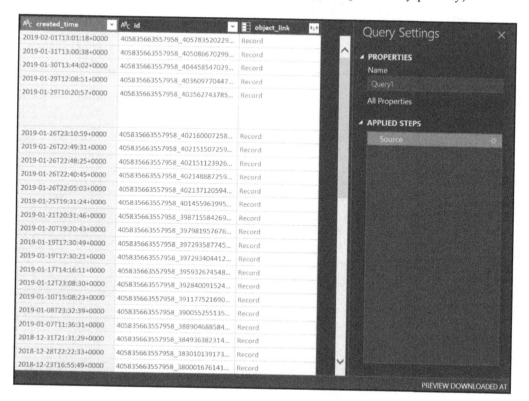

5. As we can see, the date and times of the posts are concatenated in a single column. To split this column, click on **Edit**.

6. Select the column and then **Split Column** in the **Query Editor**.

7. In the dialog, specify that you want to split the column by the character, T, as shown in the following screenshot:

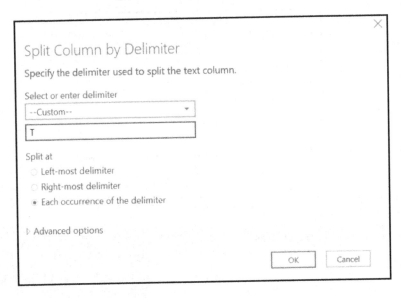

8. As a result, you get two new columns, one for the date and another one for the time, as shown in the following screenshot:

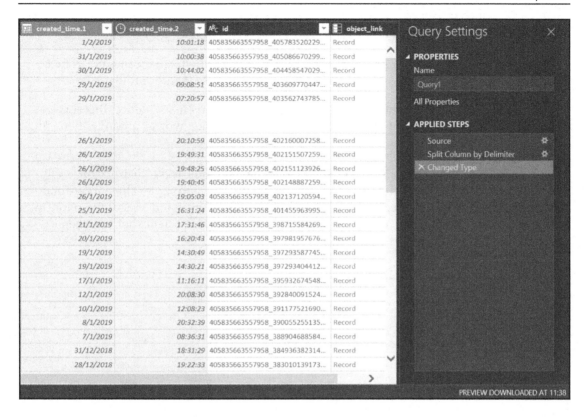

You have successfully extracted information from your Facebook page, which you can now use to analyze how often you are publishing, what type of content you are publishing, and other useful insights. This is especially useful if you are looking at a commercial profile, where you might want to adapt the content to improve the marketing of your service or product.

# Importing data from a JSON file

JSON is a standard format for sharing data, since it uses text fields that can be read by a human being. It is used by most web applications for data input and output.

In our example, we will use the Azure Text Analytics API. Given a sentence, this service can identify the text sentiment and the language and extract keywords, among other things.

The input sentence is `I had a wonderful trip to Seattle and enjoyed seeing the Space Needle!`. The API correctly identifies the language as English, extracts the main keywords, and tells us that the sentiment is positive (assigning a value larger than 0.5). All of this information is given in JSON format on the right-hand side of the window, and is available in the file we are going to import. The following screenshot has been extracted from the Azure Text Analytics demonstration page:

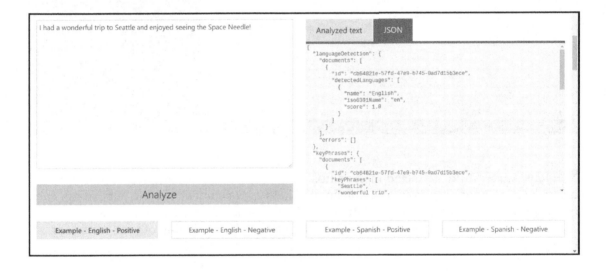

To load the input JSON file, follow these steps:

1. Click on **Data.**
2. Navigate to **Get Data** | **From File** | **From JSON**, as shown in the following screenshot:

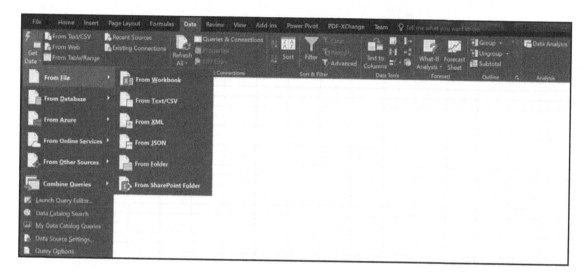

3. You will get a preview showing the main fields in the JSON structure, as shown in the following screenshot:

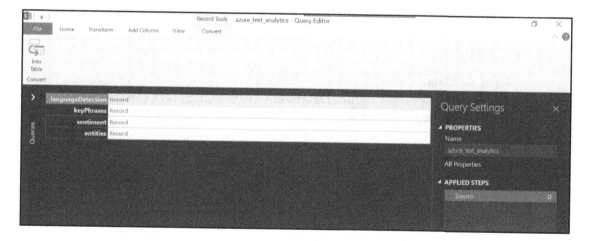

4. Click on **Into Table** to convert the entries into regular Excel tables, as shown in the following screenshot:

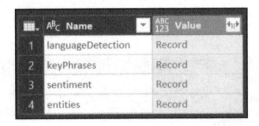

The `Value` column is a special table column that contains nested values. To navigate to the desired variable, we need to click on the ⬍ symbol and repeat this operation in the columns that will successively appear. By doing, this we can, for example, get to the sentiment value, which is 0.97. Once there are no more columns to expand, we can load the data and create a regular Excel table that contains all of the values in the JSON structure, which will be used for further analysis.

# Importing data from a database

There are many different databases available, and Excel can connect to most of them. The connection procedure is similar for all of them. We are going to use one as an example: the MS SQL Server Express database, which is free and can be downloaded on any computer. It has some limitations, but it is extremely useful for learning and testing with small amounts of data. Assuming there is a local database in your computer, perform the following steps to connect the database:

1. Click on **Data.**
2. Navigate to **Get Data | From Database | From SQL Server Database**, as shown in the following screenshot:

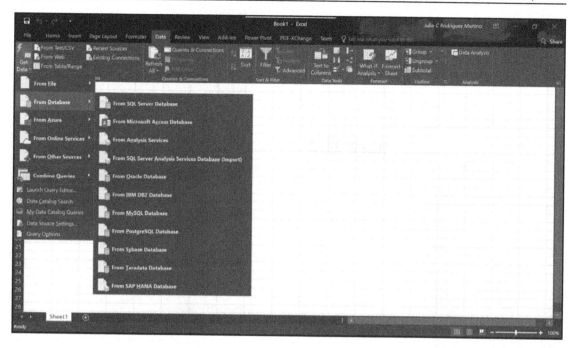

3. The pop-up dialog will request the name of the database server. In this case, it is the local computer name and the SQL Express Server. Optionally, we can add the database name, but if we leave it blank, we will be able to see a list of all databases in the server. These details are shown in the following screenshot:

4. Connect to the database using your credentials. It could be that you can log in with your Windows username and password (as shown in the following screenshot) or that you have a special username and password pair for the database:

5. If the connection is successful, you will see a list of all databases on the server and the tables contained in each database.

6. Select one of the tables and get the usual preview, as shown in the following screenshot:

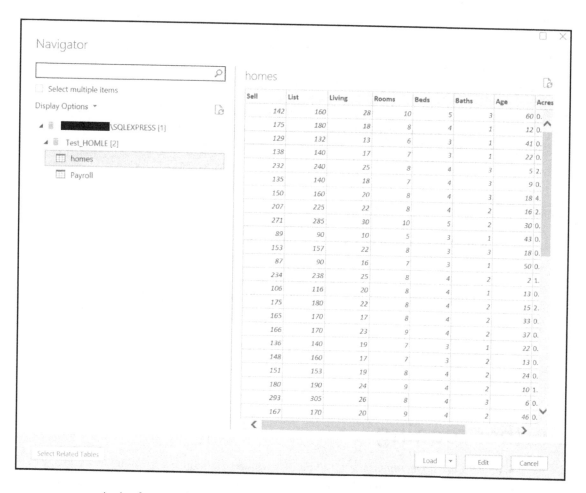

**TIP**

As in the previous cases, you can choose between editing the data or loading it. The final result will always be an Excel table.

Now, you know how to connect your Excel sheet to a database, which is the most commonly used way of storing data. Now that we have the data, the next step is to prepare it for analysis. This will be shown in detail in the next chapter.

# Summary

In this chapter, we described different methods of inputting information into an Excel spreadsheet, going beyond what can be done by hand-typing data. A variety of file types, web data sources, and databases can be analyzed from within Excel by using Power Query and Query Editor to extract, transform, and load data. I encourage you to explore other data sources, since the loading procedure is very similar.

So far, we have seen some very simple data transformations being applied to the data before it was loaded. In the next chapter, we will discuss more advanced techniques for cleansing data.

# Questions

1. Which characters can be used as separators in a text file?
2. Why is it so important to pre-process the data before loading it?
3. What is the difference between opening an Excel file and importing it?
4. What type of information can be imported from a web page?
5. JSON is one of the structured formats that's used to exchange information. What other formats exist?
6. Do some online research to understand the advantages of using databases over individual data files.

# Further reading

- *Power Query Documentation*: https://docs.microsoft.com/en-us/power-query/
- *Introduction to the Query Editor (Power Query)*: https://support.office.com/en-us/article/introduction-to-the-query-editor-power-query-1d6cdb63-bf70-4ae8-a7d5-6ae9547004d9
- *Introducing JSON*: https://www.json.org/

# 4
# Data Cleansing and Preliminary Data Analysis

After acquiring the right data, the most difficult and time-consuming task is getting it ready for analysis. Understanding what can and cannot be done with a given dataset is the first step before any model can be used. This chapter demonstrates how to use Excel functions to search and replace patterns, and how to find wrong data types and missing data. It also contains some useful diagrams so that we can get insights from the data and understand the different variables.

In this chapter, we will cover the following topics:

- Cleansing data
- Visualizing data for preliminary analysis
- Understanding unbalanced datasets

## Technical requirements

You will need to download the `titanic.xls` file from the GitHub repository at https://github.com/PacktPublishing/Hands-On-Machine-Learning-with-Microsoft-Excel-2019/tree/master/Chapter04.

# Cleansing data

Data is never clean – it always contains missing values, errors, incorrect formats, and other problems that make it impossible to feed to a machine learning model without preprocessing. This is what data cleansing is all about – correcting all these problems before starting the real analysis.

As an example of how to clean a dataset, we will use the Titanic passengers dataset. We will repeat the procedure described in the *Importing data from another Excel workbook* section of the previous chapter, to import data from an Excel workbook. We will use real data from the Titanic passengers and demonstrate how you can prepare it for analysis.

To clean a dataset, perform the necessary steps, as follows:

1. Navigate to **Data** | **From File** | **From Workbook**, as shown in the following screenshot:

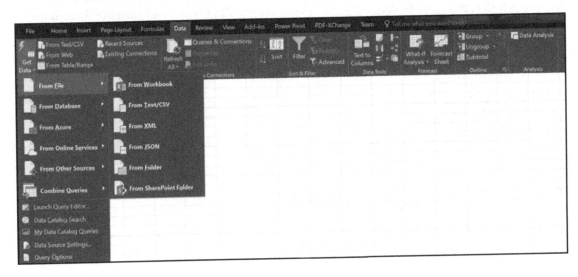

2. After selecting the `titanic.xlsx` file and the `Passenger data` worksheet, we get a preview of the file's contents, as shown in the following screenshot:

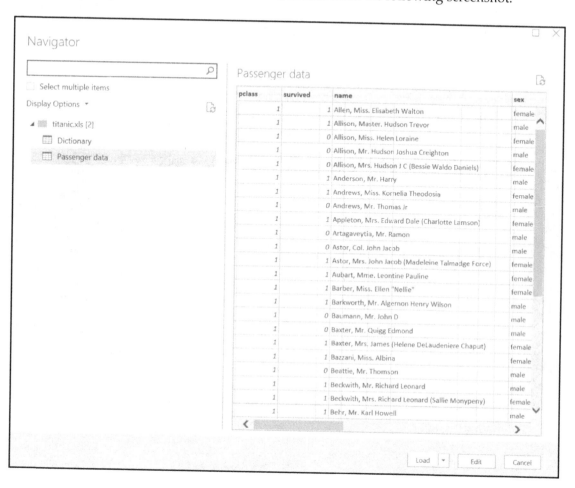

3. Click on **Edit** and start the data cleansing process. The first thing we notice is that we don't need the column containing the passenger names; it gives no useful information to our analysis. In fact, in most cases, we will be required to remove personal information from our data, due to privacy policies.

4. Select the `name` column.

5. Click on **Remove Columns**; the resulting table will look as follows:

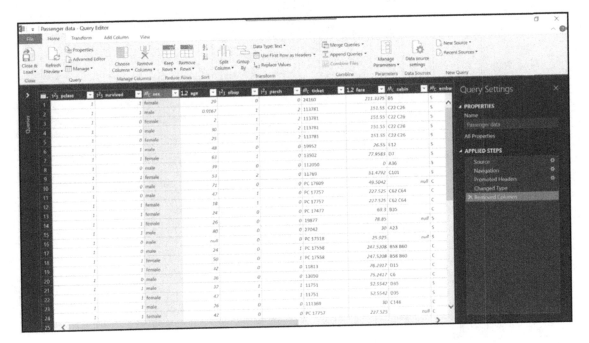

6. Replace all `nulls` in the `cabin` column with `unknown`:

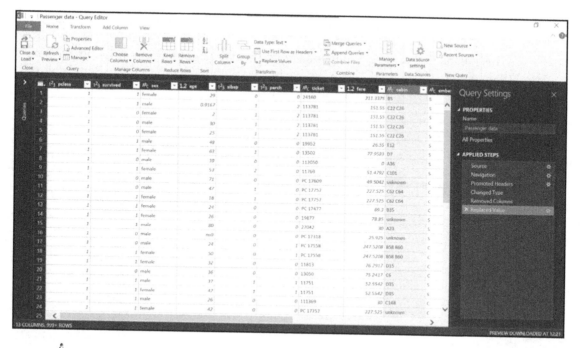

There are two other columns that contain missing values: boat and body. According to the data dictionary, they tell us which lifeboat the passenger was located in (if they survived), and which ID was assigned to their body in the case of their death. There are missing values, but there are also some cases where we cannot have a value; clearly, a dead passenger did not use a boat and a surviving passenger body was not identified. We will use some functions to account for these options.

7. In **Query Editor**, select the **Add Column** tab.
8. Select **Custom Column**.
9. The dialog shows us an option to name the new column and define its contents. Type `boat_corrected` into the textbox.

10. Define a function to calculate the column's contents, as follows:

*if [survived]=1 and [boat] = null then "unknown" else [boat]*

This means that if the passenger survived and the boat name is missing, we set the value to `unknown`. Otherwise, we just copy the value into the original column, as demonstrated in the following screenshot:

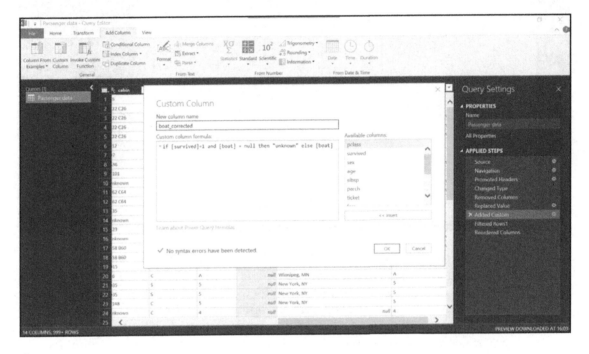

11. Add another new column in order to correct the values in `body` and define a different value for the column:

*if [survived]=0 and [body] = null then "not recovered" else [body]*

In this case, we want to say that if the passenger did not survive the shipwreck and there is no body ID, then it was probably not recovered from the water.

The result, after reordering the columns, is as follows:

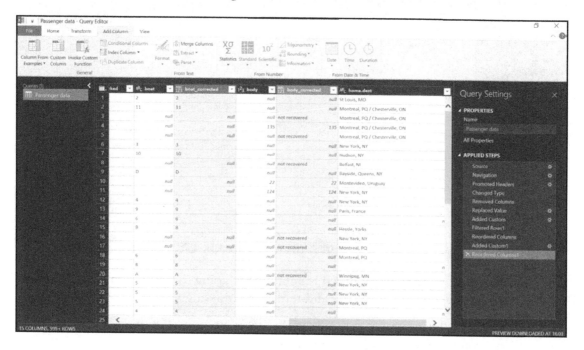

There are still `null` values in the new columns; they correspond to the preceding cases (that is, the dead passenger with no boat, or the survivor with no body ID). Replace these values with `N/A`; the resulting table is shown in the following screenshot:

The last column to be modified is `age`. We are going to simplify this by grouping the passengers into age range and replace the missing values.

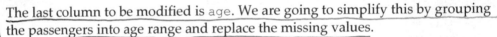

12. Replace all the missing values (`null`) with `-1`. We can do this easily by selecting the column and clicking on **Replace Values**.

13. Navigate to the **Add Column** tab.

14. Click on **Conditional Column** and define several groups, depending on the age range, as demonstrated in the following screenshot:

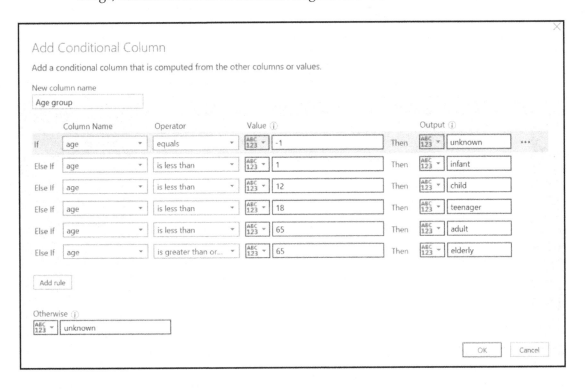

The result is a new column (`Age group`) that contains the different age groups instead of the age value and replaces the `null` values with `unknown`. The resulting table is as follows:

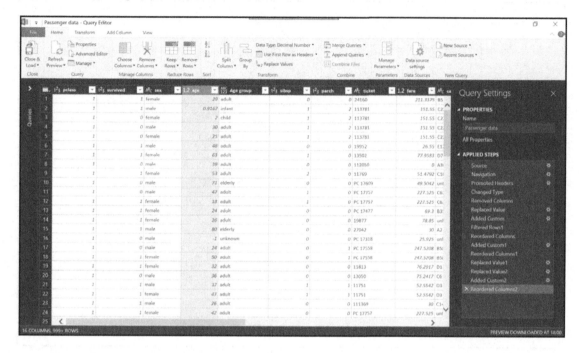

Our dataset is now clean and ready for some preliminary analysis, which we will show in the next section.

# Visualizing data for preliminary analysis

After cleaning the dataset, it is always recommended to visualize it. This helps us gain an understanding of the different variables, how their values are distributed, and the correlations that exist between them (we will explore correlations in more detail in the next chapter). We can determine which variables are important to our analyses, which ones give us more information, and which ones can be discarded for being redundant.

We will start by looking a several bar plots, where we will either count the number of occurrences of each value (using a histogram), or we will show the percentage of each value with respect to the total (using a bar plot). To achieve this, perform the following steps:

1. Right-click on any cell within the table to access the **Quick Analysis** option:

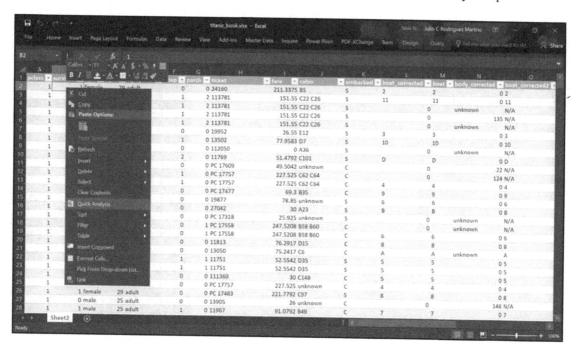

2. In the pop-up window, we can choose the chart type. Select **Clustered Column**, as shown in the following screenshot:

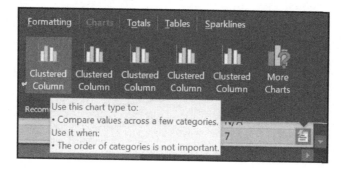

By default, Excel creates a pivot table showing some variables; we need to change the variables and the grouping operation to reflect what we need.

3. In the lower-right corner, we will see a window labeled Σ. Inside it, we can click on the variable and display the menu, as shown in the following screenshot:

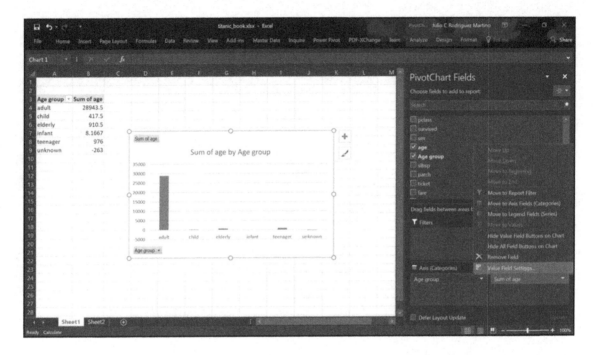

4. Click on **Value Field Settings**; you will see a pop-up window, similar to the one in the following screenshot, where you can change from **Sum** to **Count**, since we want to **Count** the values, and then calculate the **Sum** of them:

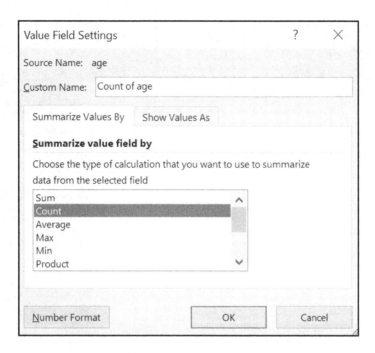

We converted the Age variable into Age group, so that is the variable that we now want to use. That is, we want to count how many passengers there are in a given age group.

5. Change the selection in **PivotChart Fields** to `Age group`.

6. Now, change the chart title and move it so that it looks similar to the following screenshot:

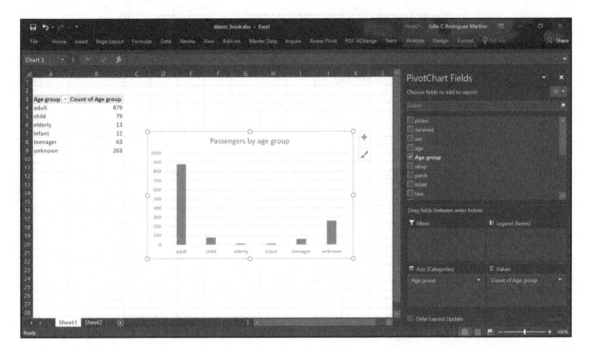

We can see that most of the listed passengers are adults. We have missing information for many of the passengers in the list, and the rest of the groups share a small number of passengers. The table that is used in the chart can be seen in the top-left corner.

An interesting question to ask is, *Is there any difference in the survival probability for different age groups?* To answer this, we need to add the `survived` variable to the **Axis (Categories)** window, which is available at the bottom right-hand corner of the sheet. We do this by dragging the variable from the **PivotCharts Fields** window and dropping it into **Axis**. The resulting chart is as follows:

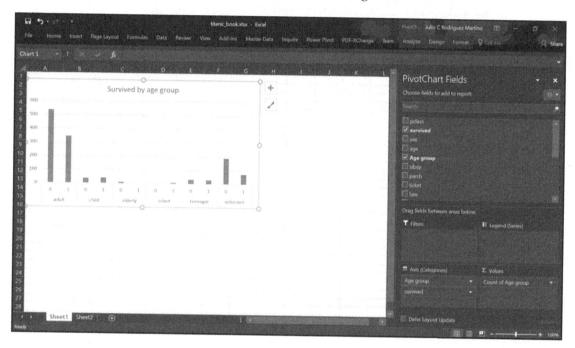

There's a notable problem with this chart – we cannot easily compare the age groups since their members are very different in number. The solution is to refer everything to the total number of passengers in each age group and show percentages instead. Looking at the previous chart, we can see that the data is grouped first by `Age group`, and then by `survived`. The first one is the parent variable. Repeat the steps we described previously to navigate to the **Value Field Settings** menu; you will see a pop-up window like the one that's shown in the following screenshot:

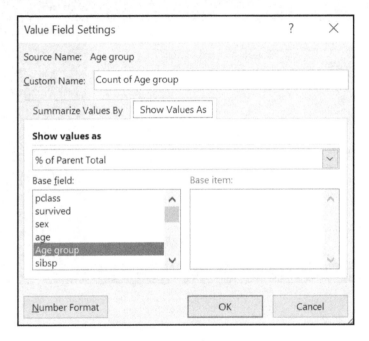

7. Click on the **Show Values As** tab, as shown in the preceding screenshot.
8. Choose the **% of Parent Total** option and the `Age group` field as the parent; the result is shown in the following screenshot:

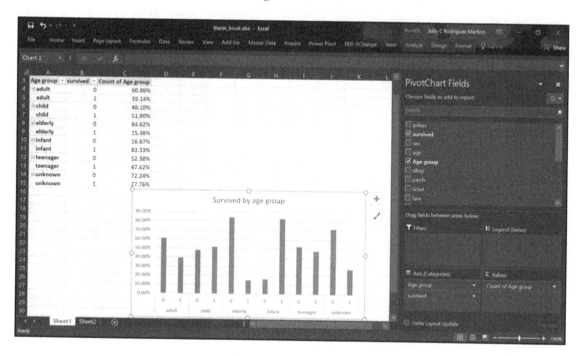

The percentage is relative to the total number of passengers within each age group, and it is now easier to compare. A large percentage of the elderly group did not survive the shipwreck, most adults suffered the same fate, and the numbers for children and teenagers seem even. It is also clear that most infants survived, probably because they were given priority to board the lifeboats.

Repeating the same steps, we can assume that it was more probable for passengers travelling in first class to survive compared to other passengers; consider the following chart:

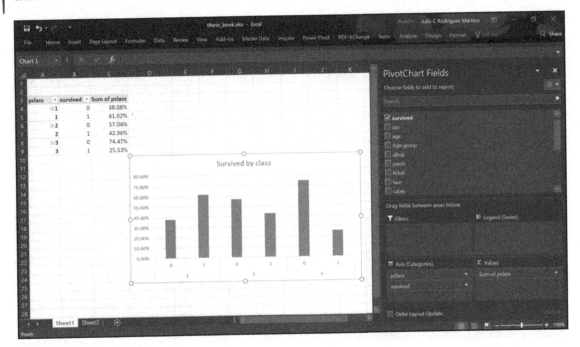

Yes, it was easier to survive if you traveled first class than if you were in third. This is a known fact about the Titanic tragedy, and we can see it reflected in the data. Travel conditions were very different in different classes, as well as safety measures.

Now, what about gender? Does it matter if the passenger was a man or a woman? Let's build a histogram of the number of men and women that survived and use it to answer our question. The resulting chart is shown in the following screenshot:

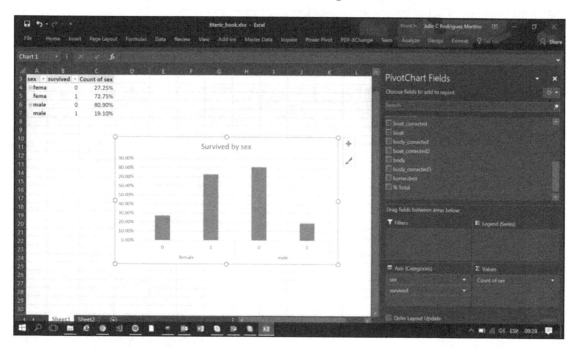

As you can see, gender clearly matters. The women survivors have a higher probability than men, at least in general terms. The reason for this might be because women were given priority to board the lifeboats, while the men, especially the young ones, were delayed in order to help other passengers, and so they couldn't make it to the lifeboats in time.

We have used a combination of the previous knowledge of our dataset and information from the data to better understand what we can and cannot do with it. You are encouraged to create diagrams for other variables and combinations, and try to understand the results. It is extremely important to understand the basic details of a dataset in order to understand whether the result we obtain from the machine learning models make sense.

# Understanding unbalanced datasets

To be able to compare the results of different variables, we need to take into account the different number of samples of each class. Let's suppose that we want to train a machine learning model to predict whether a given passenger would survive, based on age group, gender, and class. If we plot the distribution of values in the survived variable, we will see the following:

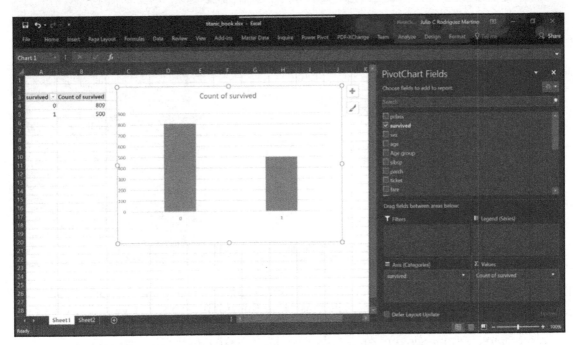

It is clear from the preceding diagram and table that there are nearly twice as many non-survivors than survivors. If we use this dataset as is, we are introducing a bias to our dataset that will affect the results. Predicting 0 for the survival variable will be approximately two times more probable than predicting 1. An exception to this statement are decision trees and their related predictive models (such as random forests and XGBoost), which can correctly deal with unbalanced datasets. Other models, especially neural networks, are very sensitive to uneven datasets. Race, gender, and other biases in algorithms raise concerns about the wide use of **Artificial Intelligence (AI)** to make decisions at all levels. This is a serious problem when applying AI to real life, and possible solutions to prevent it are still under study.

Given enough data entries, an easy way to balance the dataset is to randomly choose a number of entries from the majority class that is equal to that of the minority class. In this case, we might choose 500 rows from the rows that show survivor as 0. Let's do that using the following steps:

1. Filter the entries, as shown in the following screenshot:

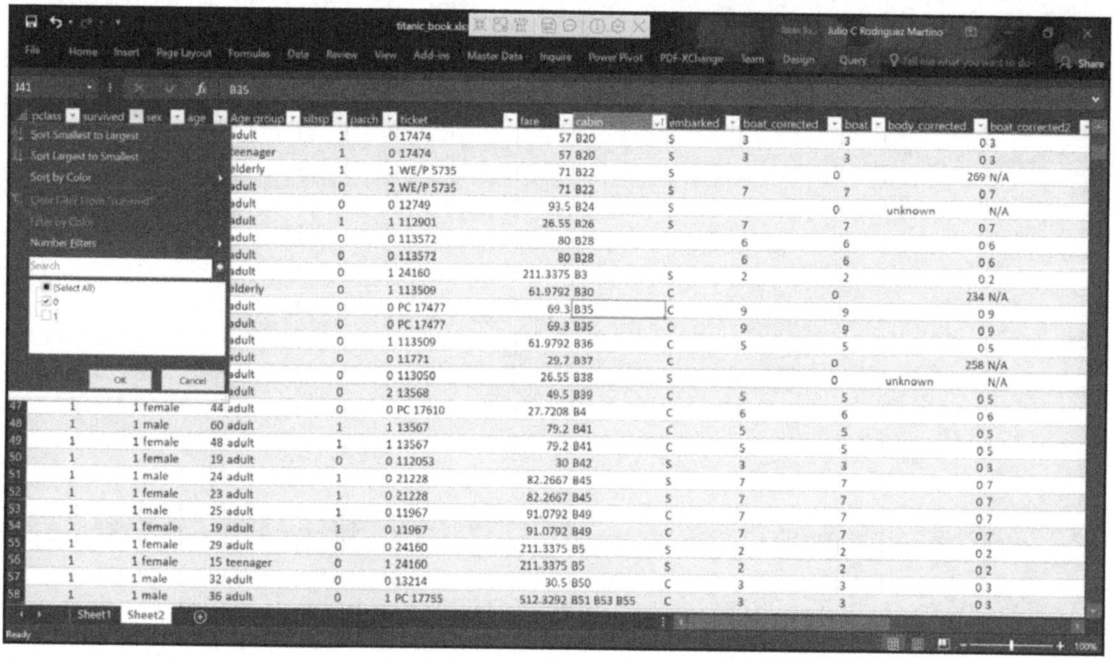

2. Copy the entries and paste them into a new worksheet.
3. Insert a new column at the beginning, named ID.
4. Turn the data into a table (**Insert | Table**, keeping the first row as headers).
5. Enter the following formula in the first cell and copy it into the rest of the column:

   =RAND()

6. Make sure that the automatic calculation is switched off. To do this, navigate to **Formulas | Calculation Options** and check **Manual**. This will prevent the random numbers from changing automatically:

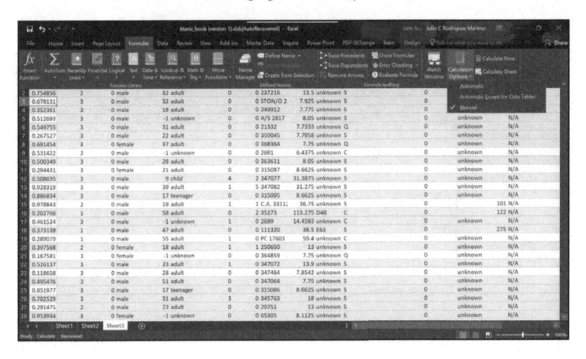

7. Order the data by ID (you can choose ascending or descending order, it does not make any difference).
8. Select the first 500 rows to be your random sample.
9. Copy these rows to a new sheet.
10. Add the 500 rows with `survived` as `1`.

You have now a perfectly balanced dataset containing 1,000 entries, which you can now use to train your machine learning model.

→ DELETE ID COLUMN FIRST

# Summary

In this chapter, we explored different methods of dealing with missing data and learned how to group or summarize it. We have shown you how important it is to visualize the data after cleaning, in order to be able to understand and interpret the results, from basic to more advanced model predictions. This is the beginning of any feature engineering, since we transform and/or discard features based on their values. Too many missing values will imply that we cannot use that variable (or feature), or a high correlation will imply that we can discard one of the correlated variables. We will dive deeper into correlations in the next chapter, showing you how to measure them quantitatively, using different methods.

Preliminary data visualization is extremely important to gain an understanding of data properties and to interpret the results we obtain, even after applying a machine learning model.

# Questions

1. Reviewing what was explained in the previous chapter, build a decision tree using `class`, `gender`, and `Age group` as features, and `survived` as the target variable. You should be able to define some conditions for a passenger to survive.
2. What variables in the dataset do you think are highly correlated?
3. Suppose that the dataset contains a numerical variable with only a few missing values. Is it possible to replace these missing values with numerical values? What value would you use?
4. Explain what bias means and why it is important to avoid it.
5. What other types of diagrams could be use for preliminary data analysis? Try some of them in the given dataset.

# Further reading

- *Best Practices in Data Cleaning: A Complete Guide to Everything You Need to Do Before and After Collecting Your Data, 1st Edition,* by Jason W. Osborn
- *Introduction to Data Visualization Techniques Using Microsoft Excel 2013 & Web-based Tools,* by Tufts Data Lab
- *Analysing the Classification of Imbalanced Data-sets with Multiple Classes: Binarization Techniques and Ad-Hoc Approaches for Preprocessing and Cost Sensitive Learning,* by A. Fernández, V. López, M. Galar, M.J. del Jesus and F. Herrera

# 5
# Correlations and the Importance of Variables

Correlation between variables, in general, means that a change in one variable reflects on the other. However, it does not mean that the change in one variable is *caused* by the change in the correlated variable. For example, the selling price of a product is correlated to its manufacturing cost, but the price increase is not totally caused by it, since there are other factors such as transportation and inflation to take into account.

Not every variable or feature in a dataset is useful for the analysis that we are planning and, sometimes, many of them are redundant. Strong correlations between pairs of variables tell us which ones can be discarded and which ones are important to predict or explain the target variable.

Different correlation calculations can be performed in Excel and used to determine the relative importance of the input features. We will show some of them in this chapter, together with graphical methods.

The dataset that will be used in this chapter has been taken from the StatLib library, which is maintained at Carnegie Mellon University, and relates the different variables of a car to its fuel consumption.

In this chapter, we will cover the following topics:

- Building a scatter diagram
- Calculating the covariance
- Calculating the Pearson's coefficient of correlation
- Studying the Spearman's correlation
- Understanding least squares
- Focusing on feature selection

# Technical requirements

You will need to download the `auto-mpg.xlsx` file from the GitHub repository at `https:/ /github.com/PacktPublishing/Hands-On-Machine-Learning-with-Microsoft-Excel-2019/tree/master/Chapter05`.

# Building a scatter diagram

First, load the `auto-mpg.xlsx` file. We will use the data in it to illustrate different aspects of this chapter. The meaning of the variables are described in the Excel file and in its references.

The simplest way of assessing correlations between variables is to create a scatter diagram, taking all features in pairs. If we plot, for example, the `Cylinders` variable in the *x* axis against the `Displacement` variable in the *y* axis, we will see a *positive correlation* (that is, the greater the number of cylinders the higher the displacement value). This is to be expected, since the calculation of the engine displacement, here expressed in cubic inches, is linearly dependent on the number of cylinders.

The scatter diagram can be seen in the following diagram:

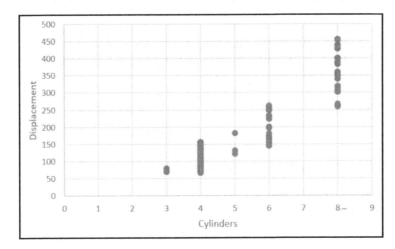

If we, instead, look at the relationship between fuel consumption and car weight, the diagram will be similar to the following:

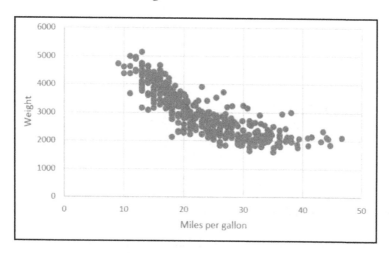

In this case, there is a negative correlation between the weight of the car and the number of miles per fuel gallon (that is, the heavier the car, the fewer number of miles it can run on a gallon of fuel). We also notice that the correlation is non-linear, meaning that a straight line will not describe the relationship between these variables.

So, what if we plot two uncorrelated variables? Could there be any correlation between, for example, the number of cylinders in the engine and the year that the car was manufactured? Let's take a look at the following diagram:

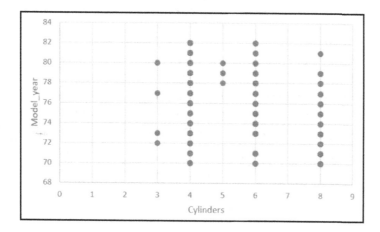

Here, we notice that cars with **3** or **5** cylinders were not very common in the time period that we are analyzing, as there are only a few examples of them. Years **78** to **80** seem to be the 5-cylinder engine period, but, apart from these facts, there were also 4-, 6-, and 8-cylinder engines being produced for each year of our dataset. There is no clear correlation between these two variables, and one of them cannot give us any information about the other.

This method of finding correlations in scatter diagrams is fine if we have a few variables, but the number of diagrams needs scales fast. In fact, if the number of variables is $N_v$, then the number of combinations needed to see all correlations is as follows:

$$N_v * (N_v - 1)$$

Even with a small dataset such as ours, to include 8 numerical variables, we need 28 diagrams to cover all the possible combinations. If we were to have hundreds of variables, then the task of finding which variables are correlated by eye is simply impossible. In the next section, we will describe methods to automatically calculate correlations, making it possible to deal with big datasets and a large number of features.

# Calculating the covariance

We need to define a statistical method that quantitatively measures the degree of association between two features. The covariance of two variables does exactly that, so let's see how it is calculated. If there are two variables, $x$ and $y$, we first center their values around their mean values, $\hat{x}$ and $\hat{y}$; then, we multiply the new values and take the mean of the product:

$$Cov(x, y) = mean[(x - \hat{x}).(y - \hat{y})]$$

This definition implies that if both variables increase or decrease at the same time, then the covariance is positive, whereas if they move in opposite directions, then the covariance is negative. If there is no correlation, the covariance value will be small, that is, close to zero.

It is also clear from the definition that, since the variables keep their scale, it is difficult to compare features that have very different mean values and it is impossible to compare two covariances.

It is easy to calculate covariances in Excel by using the **Data analysis** add-in (we explain how to activate it in the Appendix).

To calculate the covariances, perform the following steps:

1. Open the data file.
2. Navigate to **Data | Data Analysis**.
3. In the pop-up window, select **Covariance**, as shown in the following screenshot:

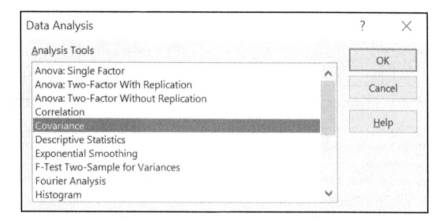

4. Select the data range; in this case, it is the whole table except the last column, which contains the car name and is non-numeric:

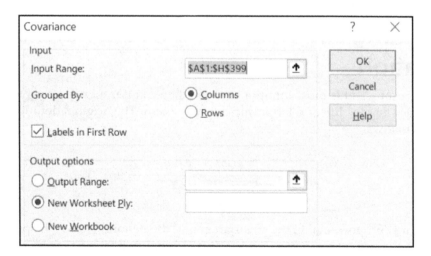

The result is the following table:

| | A | B | C | D | E | F | G | H | I |
|---|---|---|---|---|---|---|---|---|---|
| 1 | | *mpg* | *cylinders* | *displacement* | *horsepower* | *weight* | *acceleration* | *model_year* | *origin* |
| 2 | mpg | 60.93611929 | | | | | | | |
| 3 | cylinders | -10.28300927 | 2.886146 | | | | | | |
| 4 | displacem | -653.7555781 | 168.1995 | 10844.88207 | | | | | |
| 5 | horsepow | -233.2613494 | 55.20705 | 3604.81427 | 1477.789879 | | | | |
| 6 | weight | -5491.379555 | 1287.453 | 82161.4674 | 28193.51406 | 715339.1287 | | | |
| 7 | acceleratic | 9.036168531 | -2.36489 | -155.9401792 | -73.00026551 | -972.4495158 | 7.585740575 | | |
| 8 | model_ye | 16.69909977 | -2.18799 | -142.3585516 | -58.88582882 | -957.5344183 | 2.930722709 | 13.63808995 | |
| 9 | origin | 3.523310017 | -0.76555 | -50.83693594 | -14.07673886 | -393.647774 | 0.45420949 | 0.534443575 | 0.641676 |
| 10 | | | | | | | | | |

We can see a positive covariance value between `displacement` and `cylinders`, and a negative value between `weight` and `mpg`. We cannot say much more, since comparing the values is impossible, as we explained previously. The big change here is that we calculated all that values at the same time, and so we don't need to watch the diagrams one by one. The matrix is symmetrical, so only one half is shown.

There is a way to quantify correlations and compare them, and it was developed by Karl Pearson in the 1880s. Let's explore it in more detail in the next section.

# Calculating the Pearson's coefficient of correlation

The Pearson's coefficient is most commonly used when comparing two variables and it works by measuring the linear relationship between them. The original definition given by Pearson is as follows:

$$\rho_{x,y} = \frac{\sum_i (x_i - \hat{x})(y_i - \hat{y})}{\sqrt{\sum_i (x_i - \hat{x})^2 (y_i - \hat{y})^2}}$$

The numerator is proportional to the covariance, and the denominator is the product of the standard deviations ($\sigma$) of the centered variables. This normalization ensures that the limits in the possible values of $\rho$ are *-1* and *1*.

We can repeat the steps outlined in the *Calculating the covariance* section to calculate the Pearson correlation in Excel by selecting **Correlation** in the pop-up window.

The resulting table is as follows:

| | mpg | cylinders | displacement | horsepower | weight | acceleration | model_year | origin |
|---|---|---|---|---|---|---|---|---|
| mpg | 1 | | | | | | | |
| cylinders | -0.7754 | 1 | | | | | | |
| displacement | -0.8042 | 0.950721 | 1 | | | | | |
| horsepower | -0.77843 | 0.842983 | 0.897257002 | 1 | | | | |
| weight | -0.83174 | 0.896017 | 0.932824147 | 0.864537738 | 1 | | | |
| acceleration | 0.420289 | -0.50542 | -0.543684084 | -0.68919551 | -0.41745732 | 1 | | |
| model_year | 0.579267 | -0.34875 | -0.370164161 | -0.416361477 | -0.306564334 | 0.288136954 | 1 | |
| origin | 0.56345 | -0.56254 | -0.609409399 | -0.455171453 | -0.581023914 | 0.205873007 | 0.180662195 | 1 |

The cells containing a value of 1 represent the linear relationship between itself and each variable. A negative correlation implies, again, that one variable increases while the other decreases, while a positive correlation implies that both variables change in the same direction.

Pearson's coefficient is good for comparing feature relationships. For example, we can see that cylinders and displacement are more linearly correlated (by the definition of displacement, in fact) than weight and mpg, even when the ones in the second pair are related.

Another definition for the Pearson coefficient is as follows:

$$\rho_{x,y} = b.\frac{\sigma_x}{\sigma_y}$$

Here, $b$ is the slope of the linear regression that best fits $x$ versus $y$, and $\sigma_i$ are the standard deviations of $x$ and $y$. This definition clearly shows that the coefficient measures the linearity of the relationship and, at the same time, how much the two features can vary.

So, what if the relationship is not linear? In the next section, we can discuss another coefficient that will help us calculate a non-linear correlation.

# Studying the Spearman's correlation

To calculate the Spearman's coefficient, we need to first rank the values of each variable, that is, the order of the values when we sort them from highest to lowest. Once we have the new table, we will calculate Pearson's $\varrho$ on it.

In a new sheet, we define the following formula in a cell:

$$=RANK.AVG(Data!A2;auto\_mpg[mpg])$$

Here, we are asking Excel to write in that cell the ranking corresponding to the first cell of the mpg column in our data table, taking into account the full range of the column. We copy the formula to the cells on the right until we complete the number of columns of the data table (8 columns). It doesn't matter if you copy the formula to an extra cell – you will just get an error message since you are out of the data table range. In a similar way, we can copy the formulas to the remaining rows until we get to row **399** (the vertical range of the data table). We can even add a title to the new columns by using the following formula:

$$=CONCAT("Rank\_";auto\_mpg[[\#Headers];[mpg]])$$

Then, we copy it to all the cells in the first row.

A sample of the table that we obtain is as follows:

| | A | B | C | D | E | F | G | H |
|---|---|---|---|---|---|---|---|---|
| 1 | Rank_mpg | Rank_cylinders | Rank_displacement | Rank_horsepower | Rank_weight | Rank_acceleration | Rank_model_year | Rank_origin |
| 2 | 283 | 52 | 75 | 94 | 109 | 362.5 | 384 | 274 |
| 3 | 337.5 | 52 | 46.5 | 35.5 | 90 | 372 | 384 | 274 |
| 4 | 283 | 52 | 65 | 56.5 | 115 | 384 | 384 | 274 |
| 5 | 318 | 52 | 84 | 56.5 | 116 | 362.5 | 384 | 274 |
| 6 | 303 | 52 | 93 | 81 | 112 | 388 | 384 | 274 |
| 7 | 337.5 | 52 | 8 | 12.5 | 34 | 390.5 | 384 | 274 |
| 8 | 356 | 52 | 4 | 5 | 33 | 395 | 384 | 274 |
| 9 | 356 | 52 | 5.5 | 7 | 37 | 396.5 | 384 | 274 |
| 10 | 356 | 52 | 2 | 3 | 25 | 390.5 | 384 | 274 |
| 11 | 337.5 | 52 | 23 | 16 | 76 | 396.5 | 384 | 274 |
| 12 | 337.5 | 52 | 24.5 | 30 | 104 | 390.5 | 384 | 274 |
| 13 | 356 | 52 | 56 | 38.5 | 100 | 398 | 384 | 274 |
| 14 | 337.5 | 52 | 16 | 56.5 | 84 | 393.5 | 384 | 274 |
| 15 | 356 | 52 | 2 | 3 | 159 | 390.5 | 384 | 274 |
| 16 | 179 | 292.5 | 274 | 188.5 | 272 | 224.5 | 384 | 40 |
| 17 | 209.5 | 145.5 | 170 | 188.5 | 196 | 195 | 384 | 274 |
| 18 | 283 | 145.5 | 167.5 | 174 | 204 | 195 | 384 | 274 |
| 19 | 223.5 | 145.5 | 162.5 | 256 | 237 | 162.5 | 384 | 274 |
| 20 | 129 | 292.5 | 331 | 235 | 325.5 | 258 | 384 | 40 |
| 21 | 145.5 | 292.5 | 331 | 391.5 | 385.5 | 19 | 384 | 114.5 |
| 22 | 164 | 292.5 | 281 | 245.5 | 218 | 89.5 | 384 | 114.5 |
| 23 | 179 | 292.5 | 289 | 214.5 | 259 | 258 | 384 | 114.5 |
| 24 | 164 | 292.5 | 299 | 188.5 | 271 | 89.5 | 384 | 114.5 |
| 25 | 145.5 | 292.5 | 246 | 113 | 295 | 350.5 | 384 | 114.5 |
| 26 | 223.5 | 145.5 | 167.5 | 214.5 | 224 | 224.5 | 384 | 274 |
| 27 | 396.5 | 52 | 27.5 | 7 | 16 | 288.5 | 384 | 274 |
| 28 | 396.5 | 52 | 75 | 11 | 30 | 224.5 | 384 | 274 |

◄ ► … | Data | Covariance | Pearson | **Ranks** | Spearman | Sheet8 ⊕

Because `horsepower` is missing some values, they cannot be ranked and so appear as `#N/A`. Since there are only a few of them, we can remove them manually. This will avoid errors when calculating the Pearson coefficient in the next step, exactly as we did before; the result is as follows:

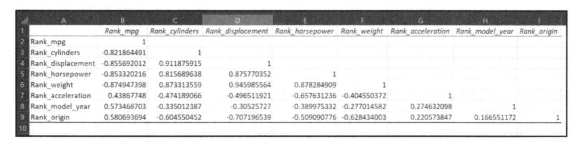

| | Rank_mpg | Rank_cylinders | Rank_displacement | Rank_horsepower | Rank_weight | Rank_acceleration | Rank_model_year | Rank_origin |
|---|---|---|---|---|---|---|---|---|
| Rank_mpg | 1 | | | | | | | |
| Rank_cylinders | -0.821864491 | 1 | | | | | | |
| Rank_displacement | -0.855692012 | 0.911875915 | 1 | | | | | |
| Rank_horsepower | -0.853320216 | 0.815689638 | 0.875770352 | 1 | | | | |
| Rank_weight | -0.874947398 | 0.873313559 | 0.945985564 | 0.878284909 | 1 | | | |
| Rank_acceleration | 0.43867748 | -0.474189066 | -0.496511921 | -0.657631236 | -0.404550372 | 1 | | |
| Rank_model_year | 0.573468703 | -0.335012387 | -0.30525727 | -0.389975332 | -0.277014582 | 0.274632098 | 1 | |
| Rank_origin | 0.580693694 | -0.604550452 | -0.707196539 | -0.509090776 | -0.628434003 | 0.220573847 | 0.166551172 | 1 |

We get similar values to that of the Pearson's coefficients, but they are slightly higher when there is a non-linear but strong correlation.

Spearman is only close to **1** if the correlation is monotonically increasing or decreasing. This is better shown in the following screenshot:

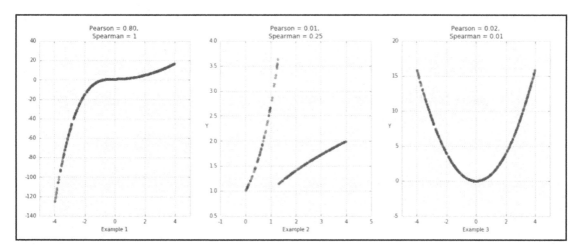

In the first diagram, Pearson is high, since the relationship can be adjusted by a straight line, even if it is not the best fit. Spearman is **1** since there is a relationship and it is monotonically increasing. The second diagram shows a relationship with an abrupt change, giving a small value for both coefficients. The third diagram shows a quadratic relationship between variables, which is neither linear nor monotonic. Looking at the three examples, we can understand that coefficients don't always give all the necessary information about the correlation between variables, but they are useful to get a general idea.

# Understanding least squares

In some instances, we might want to prove that there is a functional relationship between two variables and, hence, just use one of them in our model – since the other can be easily approximated by an expression. In this case, it is useful to rely on the least squares method. Given a set of points $(x_i, y_i)$ and a function such as $y'_i = f(x_i)$, this method minimizes the square of the differences between $y'_i$ and $y_i$. The general expression for the minimization that we are calculating is as follows:

$$min\left(\sum_i (y' - y)^2\right)$$

We will use two columns from our data table, namely `weight` and `mpg`:

1. Create a new table in a new sheet.
2. Copy the values of the `weight` and `mpg` columns.

3. Order the rows by the value of `weight`; the resulting table is as follows:

| weight | mpg |
|---|---|
| 1613 | 35 |
| 1649 | 31 |
| 1755 | 39.1 |
| 1760 | 35.1 |
| 1773 | 31 |
| 1795 | 33 |
| 1795 | 33 |
| 1800 | 36.1 |
| 1800 | 36.1 |
| 1825 | 29.5 |
| 1825 | 36 |
| 1834 | 27 |
| 1835 | 26 |
| 1835 | 40.9 |
| 1836 | 32 |
| 1845 | 29.8 |
| 1850 | 44.6 |
| 1867 | 29 |
| 1875 | 39 |
| 1915 | 35.7 |
| 1925 | 31.9 |
| 1937 | 29 |

4. Insert a line chart to see what the functional relationship looks like, as follows:

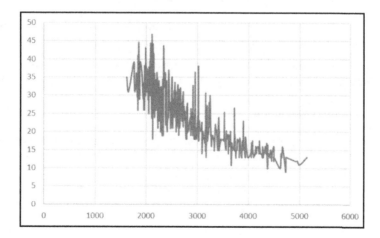

Let's say that we assume that *mpg* = *A*\*weight^(-b) and try to find the constants, *a* and *b*.

5. Create a new column, prediction, using the following formula:

=$H$2*POWER([@weight];$H$3)

The resulting table is as follows:

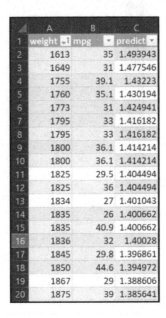

| | A | B | C |
|---|---|---|---|
| | weight | mpg | predict |
| 1 | weight | mpg | predict |
| 2 | 1613 | 35 | 1.493943 |
| 3 | 1649 | 31 | 1.477546 |
| 4 | 1755 | 39.1 | 1.43223 |
| 5 | 1760 | 35.1 | 1.430194 |
| 6 | 1773 | 31 | 1.424941 |
| 7 | 1795 | 33 | 1.416182 |
| 8 | 1795 | 33 | 1.416182 |
| 9 | 1800 | 36.1 | 1.414214 |
| 10 | 1800 | 36.1 | 1.414214 |
| 11 | 1825 | 29.5 | 1.404494 |
| 12 | 1825 | 36 | 1.404494 |
| 13 | 1834 | 27 | 1.401043 |
| 14 | 1835 | 26 | 1.400662 |
| 15 | 1835 | 40.9 | 1.400662 |
| 16 | 1836 | 32 | 1.40028 |
| 17 | 1845 | 29.8 | 1.396861 |
| 18 | 1850 | 44.6 | 1.394972 |
| 19 | 1867 | 29 | 1.388606 |
| 20 | 1875 | 39 | 1.385641 |

6. In order to fill the table, we choose the initial values of *a* = 60 (in cell *H2*) and *b* = -0.5 (in cell *H3*). These will be the starting points of the least squares method.

7. The quantity to minimize is the sum of the squares of the errors. To calculate it, we create a new column, Squared error, with the following formula;

=([@mpg]-[@prediction])^2

8. Then, use the following formula to sum all the values in that column in a cell:

=SUM(Table9[Squared error])

9. Navigate to **Data** | **Solver**; if you cannot see this option, please refer to the Appendix for instructions on how to activate **Solver**. You will see the following window pop up on your screen:

10. The **Set Objective** option is filled with the cell ID where we calculated the sum of the squared errors, and the **By Changing Variable Cells** option is filled with the ID of the two cells containing the values of *a* and *b*. We can leave the rest of the parameters as their default value settings.

11. Click on **Solve**; if the regression converges, then you will see the following window:

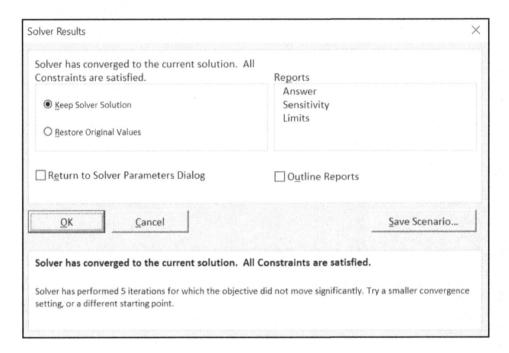

12. Choose **Keep Solver Solution** to replace the values of *a* and *b* by the ones calculated, and get new values for all predictions.

If we include the real values and the prediction in the same diagram, you should see something similar to the following screenshot:

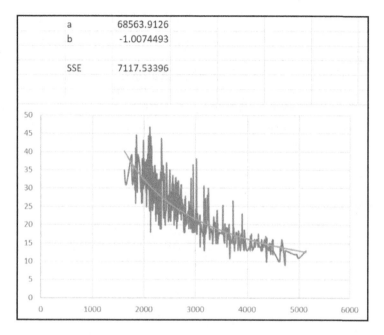

So, the adjusted function of the data points is approximately *mpg = 68564/weight*.

This adjustment is not precise due to the large dispersion in the y variable, but it could be used as a quick estimation of the fuel consumption, given the weight of the car.

We have explored a number of methods for finding correlated variables. This is useful for understanding which ones are related and which ones are redundant. The next section explains how to use this knowledge to simplify the input to our machine learning models.

# Focusing on feature selection

As we mentioned previously, none of these described methods will tell us precisely how to choose the input features by themselves. It is true that in some particular cases, if the correlations are strong enough, we could discard one or more features and just keep the ones that represent them by correlation. In general, feature engineering is a long and time-consuming task that became almost a separate field of study within machine learning.

There are automatic techniques to perform feature engineering, which are part of what is generically called **Automatic Machine Learning (AutoML)**. The method consists of letting the computer try different feature sets, including combinations of them, and test the results until the best set is found. In spite of this, there is no general recipe for selecting features, and each problem has to be analyzed—in particular, finding the set of features that lead to a better model training and predictive power.

# Summary

In this chapter, we described the most widely used methods to establish correlations between variables, which will later be used as features in a machine learning model. This is a long and difficult task, but is the basis of a good predictive model.

No method can be used alone to determine which features are important and which can be discarded. A combination of methods, plus a deep knowledge of the dataset, are fundamental to complete this task.

In the next chapter, we will leave the preliminary tasks and start focusing on some real use cases of the machine learning models.

# Questions

1. What method would be better to find a correlation between a numerical and a categorical variable?
2. Build some other plot graphs between a pair of variables and study the correlations and the logic behind them.
3. Does a negative Pearson coefficient value imply that one of the variables has negative values?
4. The table of the Pearson's coefficient can be colored or have bars added to it in order to better compare the different values. Explore these options in **Quick Analysis | Formatting**.
5. The quality of the least square regression is usually measured by the value of $R^2$. Calculate this value for the function that was adjusted in the `mpg` column versus the `weight` data value (hint: you only need to calculate one more sum of values – refer to the literature for more information).
6. The value that was calculated in the previous question should be close to 0.7, which is not good enough to prove that the function reproduces the data well. Try a different function and see what the result is.

# Further reading

- *Statistics: A Gentle Introduction*, written by Frederick L. Coolidge (refer to Chapter 6 and the references within)

# 3
# Section 3: Analytics and Machine Learning Models

Models are the core of machine learning. They can explain, predict, suggest what to do, and learn difficult tasks or time-dependent behaviors.

This section comprises the following chapters:

- Chapter 6, *Data Mining Models in Excel Hands-On Examples*
- Chapter 7, *Implementing Time Series*

# 6

# Data Mining Models in Excel Hands-On Examples

Data mining is about finding hidden patterns and associations in data. A large number of analyses that can only be performed by a human in a reasonable time if the amount of data is small, can be done by a computer in a very short time. Before Excel 2016, it was possible to install an add-in (called **Data Mining**) that was packed with different methods and models that could be used, mostly as black boxes, to get insights and discover information in any dataset. Microsoft then changed its policy and started migrating this capability to the cloud, first to Office 365 and, most recently, to Azure. It is also possible to calculate many things in Excel, with built-in functions and even with the help of macros programmed in **Visual Basic Applications (VBA)**. Here, we will show two cases where data mining can help us find important information hidden in our data.

In this chapter, we will cover the following topics:

- Learning by example: Market Basket Analysis
- Learning by example: Customer Cohort Analysis

Market Basket Analysis studies which pairs of product/services are often bought together by customers. Customer Cohort Analysis analyses which customers are still buying products/services after a given amount of time and which ones *churn*.

# Technical requirements

To complete this section, the reader will need to download the `transactions_by_dept.csv` and `cohort_input_data.csv` files from the GitHub repository at `https://github.com/PacktPublishing/Hands-On-Machine-Learning-with-Microsoft-Excel-2019/tree/master/Chapter06`.

# Learning by example – Market Basket Analysis

We have all read the sentence in almost every online store: *People who bought this product also bought....* It all started with Amazon in the 1990s, and it is widespread today. This same principle is even being tested in physical stores, where customers can get personalized suggestions on which items to buy based on their shopping history and similarity with other products. These techniques are generally known as cross-selling, and they are useful since it is often easier to sell an additional product to an existing customer than to acquire a new one.

In this section, we will show a simplified example of Market Basket Analysis, which is the type of data mining technique behind these recommender systems. The results might not be as accurate as those obtained with more advanced methods, but are still useful to explain the method and to teach how to escalate it.

We will use a list of commercial transactions downloaded from `https://data.world/`. Start by loading the `transactions_by_dept.csv` file the usual way. Navigate to **Data** | **From Text/CSV** and select the file.

You will need to edit the table in Power Query to change the data type of the first column to **Text**, since it contains the transaction ID, and will probably be interpreted as a number and truncated by Excel.

The resulting table looks like this:

| | A | B | C | D |
|---|---|---|---|---|
| 1 | POS Txn | Dept | ID | Sales U |
| 2 | 16120100160021008773 | 0261:HOSIERY | 250 | 2 |
| 3 | 16120100160021008773 | 0634:VITAMINS & HLTH AIDS | 102 | 1 |
| 4 | 16120100160021008773 | 0879:PET SUPPLIES | 158 | 2 |
| 5 | 16120100160021008773 | 0973:CANDY | 175 | 2 |
| 6 | 16120100160021008773 | 0982:SPIRITS | 176 | 1 |
| 7 | 16120100160021008773 | 0983:WINE | 177 | 4 |
| 8 | 16120100160021008773 | 0991:TOBACCO | 179 | 2 |
| 9 | 16120100160021008774 | 0597:HEALTH AIDS | 93 | 1 |
| 10 | 16120100160021008774 | 0604:PERSONAL CARE | 100 | 5 |
| 11 | 16120100160021008775 | 0819:PRE-RECORDED A/V | 135 | 1 |
| 12 | 16120100160021008775 | 0826:SMALL ELECTRICS | 138 | 1 |
| 13 | 16120100160021008775 | 0982:SPIRITS | 176 | 1 |
| 14 | 16120100160021008776 | 0961:GENERAL GROCERIES | 169 | 3 |
| 15 | 16120100160021008777 | 0982:SPIRITS | 176 | 2 |
| 16 | 16120100160021008778 | 0982:SPIRITS | 176 | 4 |
| 17 | 16120100160021008778 | 0991:TOBACCO | 179 | 1 |
| 18 | 16120100160021008779 | 0879:PET SUPPLIES | 158 | 16 |
| 19 | 16120100160021008779 | 0982:SPIRITS | 176 | 1 |
| 20 | 16120100160021008779 | 0983:WINE | 177 | 2 |
| 21 | 16120100160021008779 | 0984:BEER | 178 | 1 |
| 22 | 16120100160021008780 | 0530:SCHOOL/OFFIC SUPP | 70 | 1 |
| 23 | 16120100160021008780 | 0597:HEALTH AIDS | 93 | 1 |
| 24 | 16120100160021008780 | 0601:VALUE ZONE | 97 | 1 |
| 25 | 16120100160021008780 | 0634:VITAMINS & HLTH AIDS | 102 | 1 |

In this particular example, we will concentrate only on the first two columns. POS Txn contains the transaction ID, while Dept shows a description of the department where the transaction took place. Our goal is to find out how frequently the same customer shops in different departments in one single transaction.

In our findings we will see obvious, uninteresting combinations; unexpected ones that can be explained and exploited (for example, by offering products sold in one department when shopping in a related one), and combinations we cannot explain (which might occur by chance or simply need further investigation).

To start our analysis, we need to do the following:

1. Group all transactions by transaction number.
2. Build a list of all the departments visited in each particular purchase.

To perform these tasks, we will use the Power Query capabilities, following these steps:

1. Navigate to **Data | From Table/Range.**
2. Make sure that the data type of the POS Txn column is set to **Text** before continuing.
3. Click on **Group by**. You will see the following pop-up window:

4. Select the grouping by POS Txn, change the name of the new column to something meaningful, like Concat_dept (since we are trying to concatenate all departments visited in one purchase in a single string), and select any **Operation**. Click the **OK** button at the lower-right corner of the window, similar to the one shown in the preceding screenshot.
5. Change the calculation formula manually to get the data transformation we want. Navigate to **View** and make sure that **Formula Bar** is selected. If not, select it, and you will see the following formula:

   = *Table.Group(#"Changed Type", {"POS Txn"}, {{"Concat_dept", each Table.RowCount(_), type number}})*

The preceding formula is shown in the following screenshot:

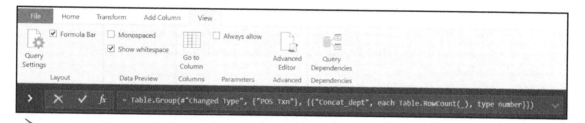

6. The formula must be replaced by the following:

*= Table.Group(#"Changed Type", {"POS Txn"}, {{"Concat_dept", each Text.Combine([Dept]," | "), type text}})*

The difference is that, instead of counting rows in the table (*Table.RowCount*), we concatenate them, using *"|"* as a delimiter (*Text.Combine*). We are also changing the output type to *text*. The output should look similar to this:

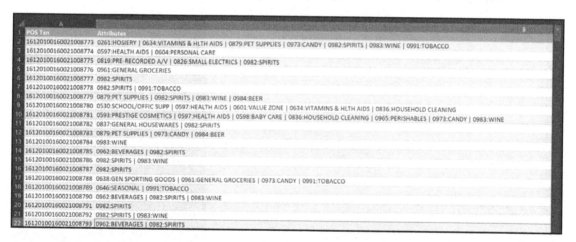

For each transaction ID, we now have a string representing the list of the departments involved. We are going to use this table to count the combinations of departments, but first, we convert it to a range:

1. Right-click on any cell within the table and go to **Table | Convert to Range**.
2. Rename the sheet to Concat depts (use the same name so that the references in future functions are correct).

In a real-life example, we might have to limit the time period we are analyzing to reduce the amount of calculations needed and clean the data, leaving out unusual transactions (outliers). In our case, we will limit the number of combinations studied. We could take the departments in pairs, triads, or even larger numbers. The problem is that the number of combinations quickly scales with the number of departments. In fact, this number can be calculated as follows:

$$N_c = \binom{m}{n}$$

Here, $m$ is the total number of elements and $n$ is the number of elements in each combination. This calculation takes into account that the elements cannot be repeated (it doesn't make sense to compare a department with itself), and the order is irrelevant.

We will select the top 10 departments according to the number of transactions and calculate the combinations using Excel functions. In order to do this, perform the following steps:

1. Create a **PivotTable** as shown in the following screenshot:

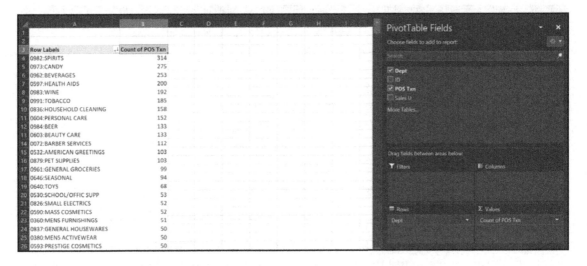

2. Order the rows by the count of transactions to get the top 10:

```
0982:SPIRITS
0973:CANDY
0962:BEVERAGES
0597:HEALTH AIDS
0983:WINE
0991:TOBACCO
0836:HOUSEHOLD CLEANING
```

```
0604:PERSONAL CARE
0603:BEAUTY CARE
0984:BEER
```

How can we easily build all possible combinations of two departments? It is simple if we define the cell contents correctly and use the copy feature built in to Excel.

Let's assume that the 10 departments are listed in cells *A1:A10*. Then follow these steps:

1. Create two new columns that you can label X and Y.
2. Define the first cell in column X as =$A$1 and the first cell in column Y as =A2.
3. Select both cells and copy them down until column Y shows an empty value. Remember that the $ symbol fixes the cell value when copying.
4. You will get a list as shown in the following screenshot, containing all possible X–Y pairs of departments:

| X | Y |
|---|---|
| 0982:SPIRITS | 0973:CANDY |
| 0982:SPIRITS | 0962:BEVERAGES |
| 0982:SPIRITS | 0597:HEALTH AIDS |
| 0982:SPIRITS | 0983:WINE |
| 0982:SPIRITS | 0991:TOBACCO |
| 0982:SPIRITS | 0836:HOUSEHOLD CLEANING |
| 0982:SPIRITS | 0604:PERSONAL CARE |
| 0982:SPIRITS | 0603:BEAUTY CARE |
| 0982:SPIRITS | 0984:BEER |

5. In the cells following the last in this list, define X as = $A$2 and Y as = A3.
6. Repeat the copy operation. If you continue until defining X as = $A$9 and Y as = A10, you will get the full list of combinations.
7. The total number of elements should be as follows:

$$N_c = \binom{m}{n} = \binom{10}{2} = \frac{10!}{2!(10-2)!} = \frac{10*9}{2} = 45$$

Going back to our `Cancat depts` sheet, we need to count the number of transactions in which each pair appears in the same transaction (X and Y) and the number of times that each department appears. We will define two functions:

1. Here, we assume that the concatenated department names are in column *B* in the `Concat depts` sheet (this is why it needs to be named like that; if you understand the function you can change the name), and columns *C* and *D* contain the X and Y list respectively. The two *COUNTIF* functions account for the fact that the department names can appear in a different order, as shown in the following formula:

   *X&Y* = =COUNTIF('Concat depts'!$B$2:$B$2065;"*"&C2&"*"&D2&"*")+COUNTIF('Concat depts'!$B$2:$B$2065;"*"&D2&"*"&C2&"*")

2. We copy the following formulas until we reach the last element, that is, number 45:

   *X* = COUNTIF('Concat depts'!$B$2:$B$2065;"*"&C2&"*")

3. We will calculate the following:

   *Support* = X&Y/N

   *Confidence* = X&Y/X

   Here, *N* is the total number of transactions. *Support* represents the frequency of the rule (combination of departments) in the data, and *Confidence* is an estimation of the conditional probability of a transaction involving the X and Y departments at the same time. Adding these two columns, we get a table as shown in the following screenshot, showing the results of the calculations:

| X | Y | X&Y | N | Support X | | Confidence |
|---|---|---|---|---|---|---|
| 0982:SPIRITS | 0973:CANDY | 31 | 2064 | 2% | 314 | 10% |
| 0982:SPIRITS | 0962:BEVERAGES | 49 | 2064 | 2% | 314 | 16% |
| 0982:SPIRITS | 0597:HEALTH AIDS | 24 | 2064 | 1% | 314 | 8% |
| 0982:SPIRITS | 0983:WINE | 77 | 2064 | 4% | 314 | 25% |
| 0982:SPIRITS | 0991:TOBACCO | 52 | 2064 | 3% | 314 | 17% |
| 0982:SPIRITS | 0836:HOUSEHOLD CLEANING | 22 | 2064 | 1% | 314 | 7% |
| 0982:SPIRITS | 0604:PERSONAL CARE | 15 | 2064 | 1% | 314 | 5% |
| 0982:SPIRITS | 0603:BEAUTY CARE | 16 | 2064 | 1% | 314 | 5% |
| 0982:SPIRITS | 0984:BEER | 50 | 2064 | 2% | 314 | 16% |
| 0973:CANDY | 0962:BEVERAGES | 67 | 2064 | 3% | 275 | 24% |
| 0973:CANDY | 0597:HEALTH AIDS | 45 | 2064 | 2% | 275 | 16% |
| 0973:CANDY | 0983:WINE | 37 | 2064 | 2% | 275 | 13% |
| 0973:CANDY | 0991:TOBACCO | 25 | 2064 | 1% | 275 | 9% |
| 0973:CANDY | 0836:HOUSEHOLD CLEANING | 35 | 2064 | 2% | 275 | 13% |
| 0973:CANDY | 0604:PERSONAL CARE | 30 | 2064 | 1% | 275 | 11% |
| 0973:CANDY | 0603:BEAUTY CARE | 31 | 2064 | 2% | 275 | 11% |
| 0973:CANDY | 0984:BEER | 16 | 2064 | 1% | 275 | 6% |
| 0962:BEVERAGES | 0597:HEALTH AIDS | 36 | 2064 | 2% | 253 | 14% |
| 0962:BEVERAGES | 0983:WINE | 24 | 2064 | 1% | 253 | 9% |
| 0962:BEVERAGES | 0991:TOBACCO | 32 | 2064 | 2% | 253 | 13% |
| 0962:BEVERAGES | 0836:HOUSEHOLD CLEANING | 27 | 2064 | 1% | 253 | 11% |
| 0962:BEVERAGES | 0604:PERSONAL CARE | 30 | 2064 | 1% | 253 | 12% |
| 0962:BEVERAGES | 0603:BEAUTY CARE | 25 | 2064 | 1% | 253 | 10% |
| 0962:BEVERAGES | 0984:BEER | 18 | 2064 | 1% | 253 | 7% |
| 0597:HEALTH AIDS | 0983:WINE | 29 | 2064 | 1% | 200 | 15% |

The calculations we have just performed are the basis of the Apriori algorithm, published by R. Agrawal and R. Srikant in 1994 for finding frequent item sets in a dataset for Boolean association rules, so named because it uses prior knowledge of frequent item set properties. The Apriori algorithm is also useful in mining frequent item sets and relevant association rules. Usually, this algorithm is used to operate on a database containing a large number of transactions, such as items that customers buy at a supermarket. It helps customers to easily make their purchases and enhances the sales performance of the store. It is important to notice that the correlation between items does not imply causation; for example, that buying one item causes someone to buy another.

In a real-world scenario, we would choose the combinations with the largest *Support* and *Confidence* above a certain threshold, and study those insights. Apart from obvious rules, such as people shopping at the spirits and wine departments in the same purchase, we will find other combinations that we didn't expect. The main point is to find actionable insights; that is, those we can do something about. We can offer new articles, combine them in promotions, and advertise them in different places.

There are a large number of possibilities. The important thing is that the machine has learned hidden associations and has given us useful information about our own business. It is extremely important that it is not only machine learning specialists who are a part of these analyses, but also people involved in the business should give their impressions and use their experience and knowledge to turn this information into an economic benefit.

Can a full analysis be carried out in Excel? Should we limit ourselves to a toy model if we don't have access to more advanced tools? Of course not! Excel is extremely powerful and able to be used in advanced analyses, but we need to know how to write a little VBA code in macros.

The concept of Market Basket Analysis should be clear now, and we can move forward to another example of customer behavior analysis.

# Learning by example – Customer Cohort Analysis

An excellent way of gaining insights about a company's customers and their behavior is to perform a segmented analysis. These segments are groups of customers that share the same characteristics and are usually called **cohorts**. Their definition depends very much on the type of business we are dealing with.

The dataset we will analyze contains a list of customer IDs, the date when they first purchased something from us, the day they left us, and the mean amount of money spent per month. What does "left us" mean in this context? It is mainly a matter of definition. For example, if we refer to a credit card, we could consider that the customer left when they cancelled the card, or maybe we want to go further and say that if the customer did not spend any money for two or three months, we consider that they have left.

Our grouping will then be based on the starting date. We will study how many customers **churned**, or abandoned us in a given period.

The **Lifetime Value of a Customer (LTV)** often refers to the gross profit generated by this customer over the whole period that they stayed with us. Both analyses together help us decide which customers we must retain and which actions were more effective in acquiring more valuable customers in terms of monthly spend and fidelity.

The analysis comprises the following steps:

1. Read the `cohort_input_data.csv` input file, navigating to **Data | From Text/CSV** and selecting it.

2. The two date columns, `Date in` and `Date out`, look better and are easier to understand if we choose the *month-year* format for them. Select the columns, right-click on them, and click on **Format Cells**. A pop-up window, like the one in the following screenshot, will appear:

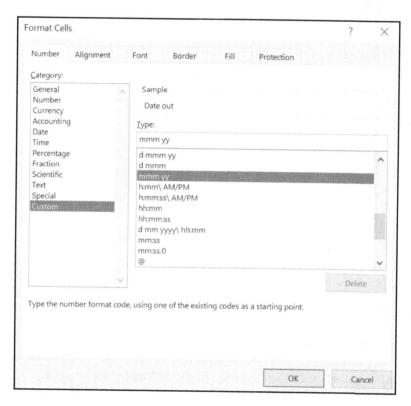

3. Add two columns: `Cohort`, which in this case is equal to `Date in`, and `Active months`, which we can calculate as follows:

   =*DATEDIF(B2;C2;"m")*

   This assumes that column *B* contains the `Data in` values and column *C* contains the `Data out` values.

4. Copy this formula to the remaining cells. The resulting table, sorted by `Date in`, is as follows:

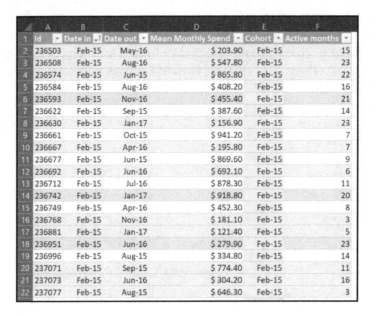

| Id | Date in | Date out | Mean Monthly Spend | Cohort | Active months |
|---|---|---|---|---|---|
| 236503 | Feb-15 | May-16 | $ 203.90 | Feb-15 | 15 |
| 236508 | Feb-15 | Aug-16 | $ 547.80 | Feb-15 | 23 |
| 236574 | Feb-15 | Jun-15 | $ 865.80 | Feb-15 | 22 |
| 236584 | Feb-15 | Aug-16 | $ 408.20 | Feb-15 | 16 |
| 236593 | Feb-15 | Nov-16 | $ 455.40 | Feb-15 | 21 |
| 236622 | Feb-15 | Sep-15 | $ 387.60 | Feb-15 | 14 |
| 236630 | Feb-15 | Jan-17 | $ 156.90 | Feb-15 | 23 |
| 236661 | Feb-15 | Oct-15 | $ 941.20 | Feb-15 | 7 |
| 236667 | Feb-15 | Apr-16 | $ 195.80 | Feb-15 | 7 |
| 236677 | Feb-15 | Jun-15 | $ 869.60 | Feb-15 | 9 |
| 236692 | Feb-15 | Jun-16 | $ 692.10 | Feb-15 | 6 |
| 236712 | Feb-15 | Jul-16 | $ 878.30 | Feb-15 | 11 |
| 236742 | Feb-15 | Jan-17 | $ 918.80 | Feb-15 | 20 |
| 236749 | Feb-15 | Apr-16 | $ 452.30 | Feb-15 | 8 |
| 236768 | Feb-15 | Nov-16 | $ 181.10 | Feb-15 | 3 |
| 236881 | Feb-15 | Jan-17 | $ 121.40 | Feb-15 | 5 |
| 236951 | Feb-15 | Jun-16 | $ 279.90 | Feb-15 | 23 |
| 236996 | Feb-15 | Aug-15 | $ 334.80 | Feb-15 | 14 |
| 237071 | Feb-15 | Sep-15 | $ 774.40 | Feb-15 | 11 |
| 237073 | Feb-15 | Jun-16 | $ 304.20 | Feb-15 | 16 |
| 237077 | Feb-15 | Aug-15 | $ 646.30 | Feb-15 | 3 |

5. Rename this sheet `Customer data` for future reference.

First, we will study how well we retained customers over the lifetime of a given cohort. Each group will tell us what actions to repeat and which to avoid to prevent customer churn. We will use the *COUNTIFS* Excel function to count the number of active customers per month in each cohort:

1. Create a matrix with 48 rows, from zero to the largest difference in months in our dataset (48 months), and one column per month, from `Feb-15` to `Jan-19`. An example of this matrix can be seen in the following screenshot:

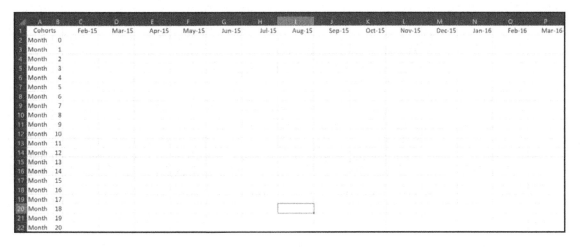

2. Add a row at the end of the table to calculate the total number of customers in each cohort by using the following formula:

   =COUNTIF('Customer data'!$E$2:$E$751;"="&C$1)

   This is because column *E* in the `Customer data` sheet contains the list of cohorts, and row one contains the list of cohorts in our matrix.

3. Copy the cell contents to all cells to the right in the table, and, since the row is fixed, the correct values are calculated for each column, as shown in the following screenshot:

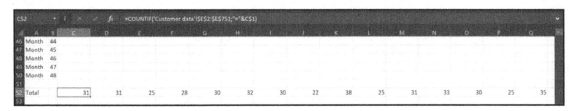

4. In the first cell of the matrix, write the following formula:

   =COUNTIFS('Customer data'!$E$2:$E$751;"="&C$1;'Customer data'!$C$2:$C$751;">"&EOMONTH(C$1;$B1))/C$52

Let's see in detail what it means:

- We only count if the contents of *C1* (Feb-15, the current cohort) are part of the list of cohorts in column *E* in the `Customer data` sheet.
- We count if `Date out` (column *C* in the `Customer data` sheet) is larger than the current cohort plus the number of months in column *B*. We use the *EOMONTH* function to deal with the fact that we might have full dates as inputs, and not just months and years. Check the definition of this function in Excel help.
- We finally divide this by the total number of customers to get a percentage.

5. Copy the formula to the whole matrix.
6. Format the cells as a percentage.
7. Format the cells conditionally using a three-color scale. The result looks like the following screenshot:

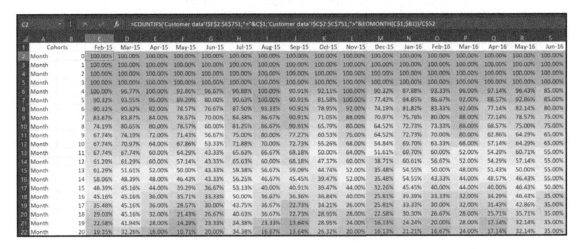

We can see, for example, that after 20 months, only 19% of the customers acquired in `Feb-15` remain. The color scale also shows that some cohorts show a faster churn than others. It is now necessary for the business expert to evaluate what actions were actions taken during each time period and repeat or change them.

We know now how many customers we were able to keep, but what was their value? They do not spend the same amount, so we need to include that variable in the analysis. Follow these steps:

1. Create a similar matrix, with the month number and cohorts, but now we will use a different formula:

   =SUMIFS('*Customer* data'!$D$2:$D$751;'Customer data'!$E$2:$E$751;"="&C$1;'Customer data'!$C$2:$C$751;">"&EOMONTH(C$1;$B1))

   This formula means that we only sum the values on the Customer data sheet in column *D* if two conditions are met:

   - If the summed values correspond to the cohort in *C1*
   - If Date out is larger than the current cohort, that is, the customer is still with us

2. Copy the cell value to the whole matrix.
3. Format the table in a similar way as before to get a colored matrix, as shown in the following screenshot:

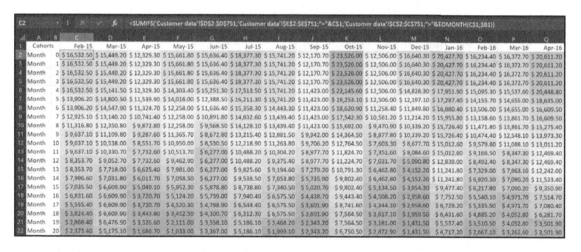

In this case, we can see how the amount of money spent changes with time for each cohort, and it is slightly different then the raw number of customers.

# Summary

In this chapter, we learned about two data mining techniques: Market Basket Analysis and Customer Cohort Analysis. The first one tells us about hidden relations between store departments or products based on the customers' behavior. The second shows the time evolution of the number of customers, revealing differences between different customer segments or cohorts.

There are a large number of data mining analyses that can help us dig into our datasets and find hidden information, which is extremely important in order for us to understand our business and make the right decisions.

In the next chapter, we will study a special kind of dataset in detail: time series. We will see that it needs a different kind of modeling and analysis.

# Questions

1. How can the unexplainable, random associations be avoided in a Market Basket Analysis?
2. If we find a correlation between two products or two departments in a given store, can this be generalized to other places?
3. Some columns in the cohort matrix show zeroes starting at a given date. What does this mean in the context of the current dataset?
4. The last rows in the cohort matrix show zero consistently. What does this mean in the context of the current dataset?
5. How would you maximize the amount of money spent by customers as time passes?

# Further reading

- *Database Marketing: Analyzing and Managing Customers* by Robert C. Blattberg, Byung-Do Kim, Scott A Neslin
- *Data Science for Business: What You Need to Know about Data Mining and Data-Analytic Thinking, 1st Edition,* by Foster Provost, Tom Fawcett

# Implementing Time Series

**7**

Time evolving phenomena are fundamental to many disciplines. Understanding what happened and foreseeing how different variables will evolve is key knowledge for making correct, informed decisions.

Time series analysis is a broad field, with many different methods to detect patterns, predict behaviors, and decompose the time evolution into known and previously studied shapes. We are going to discuss some of them, focusing on the ones that are easily solved using Excel. The idea, as usual, is that our machines learn about the details in the data and can extract useful knowledge about the past and the possible future developments.

In this chapter, we will cover the following topics:

- Modeling and visualizing time series
- Forecasting time series automatically in Excel
- Studying the stationarity of a time series

# Technical requirements

To complete this chapter, the reader will need to download the `AirPassengers_modified.csv` file from the GitHub repository at https://github. com/PacktPublishing/Hands-On-Machine-Learning-with-Microsoft-Excel-2019/tree/ master/Chapter07.

# Modeling and visualizing time series

We have seen that doing a preliminary data analysis and visualizing the dataset is the first step in any machine learning project. Time series are no exception. So, we will start by exploring time series and learning about its different characteristics.

In the case of a time series, a preliminary analysis implies *modeling* it; that is, understanding whether it is periodic, whether it shows a given tendency (increasing or decreasing with time), or whether it is stationary (mean and variance of the values don't change over time), among other measures. Visualization plays a fundamental role in this analysis, since many of the time series characteristics can be deduced using a graphical representation of the data points, even if there are numerical methods to calculate them.

Let's use a popular dataset to illustrate the modeling and visualization of a time series. The AirPassengers_modified.csv file is a simplified version of a very popular dataset, usually shown as an example when teaching time series analysis (source: *Box, G. E. P., Jenkins, G. M. and Reinsel, G. C. (1976) Time Series Analysis, Forecasting and Control. Third Edition. Holden-Day. Series G*). Our version contains the amount of international passengers (in thousands) that traveled by plane between 1949 and 1961, grouped by month. After loading the file the usual way (**Data | From Text/CSV**), we can visualize the time series in the following diagram, where we can see the number of passengers as a function of time:

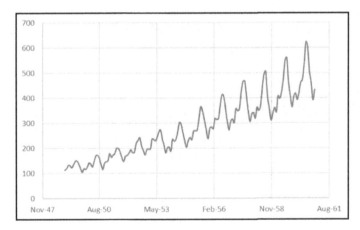

The first thing that we notice is that the number of passengers increases with time. Then, if we look carefully at the peaks in the series, there is a 12-month pattern that seems to repeat. Let's prove this observation with the data.

The easiest way to get a trend is to use Excel's built-in capability to calculate trends. To use it, follow these steps:

1. Click on the chart area.
2. Check the box for **Trendline**.
3. Click on `More Options...`, as shown in the following screenshot:

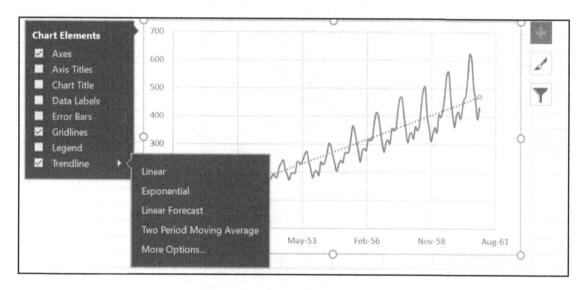

The first selection will show the line in the chart and then, after selecting **More options...**, we can check the box to see the line equation expression on the chart. Notice that **Linear** is not the only option for a trend line and that more sophisticated regressions are available, as shown in the following screenshot:

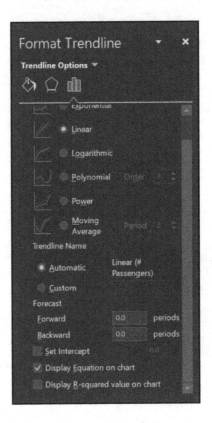

The resulting equation, as shown on the chart, is as follows:

$$Passengers = 0.0873*TravelDate - 1472$$

Looking at the resulting plot, we see that a straight line does not correctly follow the time evolution of the series. Some parts are mostly above the line and others below, as you can see in the following chart:

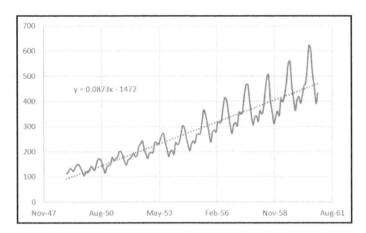

How can we model the general behavior of the dataset? We can start by realizing that we could think about the series as composed of three parts:

- A periodic part, which repeats every 12 months (we guess this because of the periodicity of the peaks, and call this 12 month period a *season*)
- An increasing part, which we can obtain by regression or averaging the series
- A *noise* part, which we basically define as the remaining values once we isolate the first two parts

This model can then be written as follows:

$$Passengers = periodic(TravelDate) * increasing(TravelDate) * noise(TravelDate)$$

Let's improve the calculation of the *increasing* part by using a moving average. This can be calculated automatically by Excel, but we will do it manually since it is simple and we can understand exactly how it works:

1. Start by calculating the average number of passengers in the first 12 months:

    =AVERAGE(B2:B13)

2. In the cell to the right, calculate the standard deviation (we will use it in the next section, when we test the stationarity of the series):

   =STDEV.S(B2:B13)

3. Copy both calculations down to the end of the table.

   We then have the mean value and standard deviation of the previous 12 months in each pair of cells. In practice, we are defining a moving 12-month window and sliding it through the data. The resulting table looks similar to the following screenshot:

| TravelDate | # Passengers | Moving average | Moving Std Dev |
|---|---|---|---|
| Jan-49 | 112 | | |
| Feb-49 | 118 | | |
| Mar-49 | 132 | | |
| Apr-49 | 129 | | |
| May-49 | 121 | | |
| Jun-49 | 135 | | |
| Jul-49 | 148 | | |
| Aug-49 | 148 | | |
| Sep-49 | 136 | | |
| Oct-49 | 119 | | |
| Nov-49 | 104 | | |
| Dec-49 | 118 | 126.6666667 | 13.72014666 |
| Jan-50 | 115 | 126.9166667 | 13.45334249 |
| Feb-50 | 126 | 127.5833333 | 13.16647487 |
| Mar-50 | 141 | 128.3333333 | 13.68697678 |
| Apr-50 | 135 | 128.8333333 | 13.82246744 |
| May-50 | 125 | 129.1666667 | 13.66370995 |
| Jun-50 | 149 | 130.3333333 | 14.76071773 |

The first 12 places are obviously empty, since we need at least 12 values to start averaging. If we show everything in the same diagram, we will see a graph similar to the following:

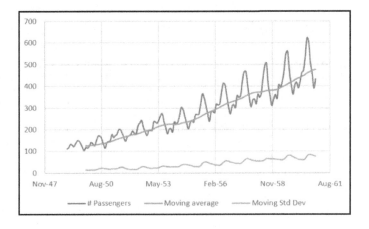

The moving average follows the details of the series better, and we are going to use it as a good approximation for *increasing(TravelDate)*. Notice that the moving standard deviation also increases with time, we will use this result in the next section.

Going back to our model for the time series, we can write:

$$\frac{Passengers}{increasing(TravelDate)} = periodic(TravelDate) * noise(TravelDate)$$

The ratio is between the column *Passengers* and the moving average calculated right before. You will be missing the first 12 points, since the average need to start somewhere, but that is fine. For the rest of the rows you can calculate *Passengers/Moving Average*, which approximates *Passengers/increasing(TravelDate)*.

4. Add an extra column to calculate this ratio.
5. Build a new diagram to show the calculation. You will see something like the following graph:

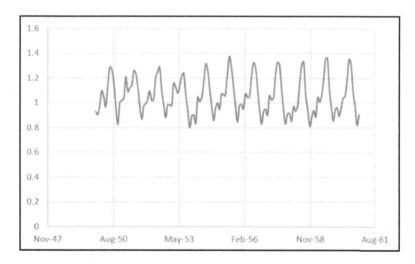

We clearly managed to extract the increasing part, but we still have a mixture of oscillations and noise. Let's model *periodic(TravelDate)* by repeating the first 12 values in sequence.

6. In a new column, copy and paste the first 12 values as many times as you need to fill the same number of cells. These values will give you the following graph:

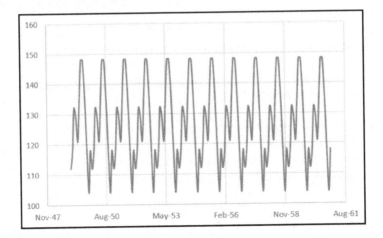

Finally, we will calculate *noise(TravelDate)*. We will, again, calculate this from our model:

$$noise(TravelDate) = \frac{Passengers}{periodic(TravelDate) * increasing(TravelDate)}$$

7. In another column, use the preceding calculation to create a new diagram:

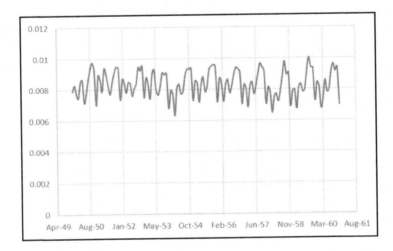

We now have a full model of the time series and we can use it to predict the future values!
Let's do it step by step:

1. Open a new sheet.
2. Copy the series values and extend the time period up to `Dec-62`.
3. In column C, copy the *periodic(TravelDate)* values (24 values in two equal series of 12 values).
4. In column D, copy the noise values corresponding to the last two years.
5. In column E, cell 146, calculate *increasing(TravelDate)* using the trendline formula (*=0.0873*A146 - 1472*).
6. Copy the formula down to the end of the table. Cell `B1` is then as follows:

    *=C146*D146*E146*

The same calculation is then copied down. The resulting table is as follows:

|  | A | B | C | D | E |
|---|---|---|---|---|---|
| 144 | Nov-60 | 390 | | | |
| 145 | Dec-60 | 432 | | | |
| 146 | Jan-61 | 418.5687 | 112 | 0.007897 | 473.22 |
| 147 | Feb-61 | 447.7342 | 118 | 0.007973 | 475.92 |
| 148 | Mar-61 | 425.3093 | 132 | 0.006735 | 478.37 |
| 149 | Apr-61 | 502.9614 | 129 | 0.008105 | 481.08 |
| 150 | May-61 | 488.2151 | 121 | 0.008342 | 483.69 |
| 151 | Jun-61 | 514.4723 | 135 | 0.007835 | 486.40 |
| 152 | Jul-61 | 576.8031 | 148 | 0.00797 | 489.02 |
| 153 | Aug-61 | 665.485 | 148 | 0.009144 | 491.73 |
| 154 | Sep-61 | 675.077 | 136 | 0.010039 | 494.43 |
| 155 | Oct-61 | 555.4341 | 119 | 0.00939 | 497.05 |
| 156 | Nov-61 | 486.2185 | 104 | 0.009355 | 499.76 |
| 157 | Dec-61 | 430.2691 | 118 | 0.007258 | 502.38 |
| 158 | Jan-62 | 477.5688 | 112 | 0.008442 | 505.08 |
| 159 | Feb-62 | 488.9317 | 118 | 0.00816 | 507.79 |
| 160 | Mar-62 | 456.3509 | 132 | 0.006776 | 510.23 |
| 161 | Apr-62 | 490.4094 | 129 | 0.007411 | 512.94 |
| 162 | May-62 | 535.7012 | 121 | 0.008587 | 515.56 |
| 163 | Jun-62 | 546.0296 | 135 | 0.007804 | 518.27 |
| 164 | Jul-62 | 614.8332 | 148 | 0.007975 | 520.88 |
| 165 | Aug-62 | 708.8846 | 148 | 0.009148 | 523.59 |
| 166 | Sep-62 | 688.351 | 136 | 0.009617 | 526.30 |
| 167 | Oct-62 | 575.2492 | 119 | 0.009139 | 528.92 |
| 168 | Nov-62 | 519.6916 | 104 | 0.0094 | 531.62 |
| 169 | Dec-62 | 439.6429 | 118 | 0.006974 | 534.24 |

7. Insert a new diagram, including the two data series, original and predicted.

8. In the following graph, you can see that the prediction is pretty good! (Or, at least it follows the historical data; the only real measure of the prediction quality is to compare it with real data for those dates):

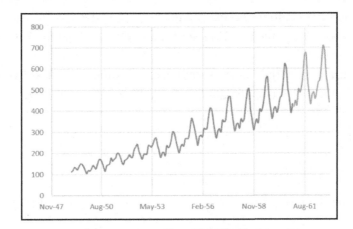

We have followed the necessary steps to model a time series based on its characteristics and extensively using calculations and visualizations. We will show in the next section that this can also be achieved automatically by using Excel's built-in capabilities.

# Forecasting time series automatically in Excel

Now that we have forecast a time series the hard way, understanding every step, we can do it the easy way. We will use Excel's built-in functions to predict the future number of passengers. Perform the following steps:

1. Select both columns, TravelDate and Passengers, corresponding to the time and number of passengers.
2. Navigate to **Data** in the main menu.
3. Select **Forecast Sheet** (see the following screenshot for reference):

4. A window will pop up, showing a preview of the forecast and giving us the chance to change some parameters by clicking in **Options**:

- **Forecast End**: We can choose the end of the forecast period. By default, Excel forecasts three seasons ahead (more on this to follow).
- **Forecast Start**: We can do the same with the start of the forecast period. Default is the last point in time of our time series.
- **Confidence interval**: This is defined as the range centered on every predicted value, in which 95% of the predicted points will fall (assuming a normal distribution of the forecast points).
- **Seasonality**: A season is the period in which a time series repeats it pattern (if it is periodic, of course). It can be added manually or detected automatically.

The following graph shows the pop-up window containing the available options:

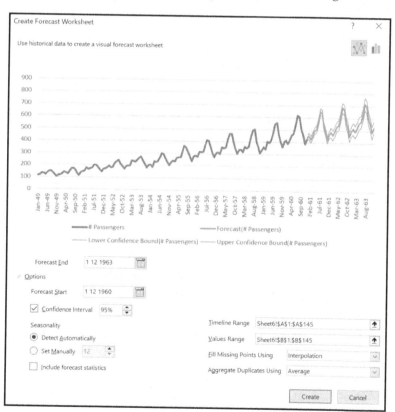

5. **Timeline Range** and **Values Range** are the selected columns (in our case `TravelDate` and `Passenger`).

6. Clicking on **Create**, we obtain three new columns: `Forecast`, `Lower Confidence Bounds (Passengers)`, and `Upper Confidence Bounds (Passengers)`:

| | TravelDate | # Passengers | Forecast(# Passengers) | Lower Confidence Bound(# Passengers) | Upper Confidence Bound(# Passengers) |
|---|---|---|---|---|---|
| 142 | Sep-60 | 508 | | | |
| 143 | Oct-60 | 461 | | | |
| 144 | Nov-60 | 390 | | | |
| 145 | Dec-60 | 432 | 432 | 432.00 | 432.00 |
| 146 | Jan-61 | | 453.8122736 | 427.08 | 480.54 |
| 147 | Feb-61 | | 427.8263121 | 400.96 | 454.69 |
| 148 | Mar-61 | | 459.262672 | 432.26 | 486.27 |
| 149 | Apr-61 | | 498.909199 | 471.76 | 526.05 |
| 150 | May-61 | | 508.8944168 | 481.61 | 536.18 |
| 151 | Jun-61 | | 569.8482444 | 542.42 | 597.28 |
| 152 | Jul-61 | | 653.6777865 | 626.10 | 681.25 |
| 153 | Aug-61 | | 637.3598214 | 609.63 | 665.08 |
| 154 | Sep-61 | | 539.05814 | 511.18 | 566.93 |
| 155 | Oct-61 | | 490.8222267 | 462.80 | 518.85 |
| 156 | Nov-61 | | 421.258682 | 393.08 | 449.44 |
| 157 | Dec-61 | | 464.425986 | 436.09 | 492.76 |
| 158 | Jan-62 | | 486.2264429 | 447.07 | 525.38 |
| 159 | Feb-62 | | 460.2404815 | 420.97 | 499.51 |
| 160 | Mar-62 | | 491.6768414 | 452.28 | 531.07 |
| 161 | Apr-62 | | 531.3233684 | 491.81 | 570.84 |
| 162 | May-62 | | 541.3085862 | 501.68 | 580.94 |
| 163 | Jun-62 | | 602.2624138 | 562.51 | 642.02 |

We will also see the following diagrams, showing the time series plus the forecasted values:

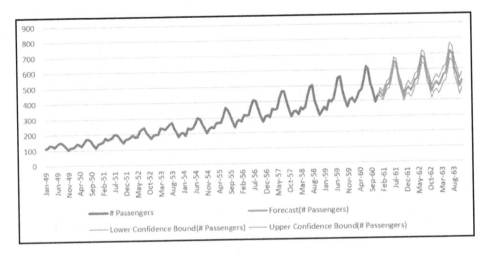

If we select **Include forecast statistics** in the pop-up window, we get the following table:

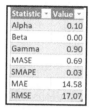

This values correspond to Excel's built-in *FORECAST.ETS.STAT* function used internally by the forecast algorithm. The meaning of these values are as follows:

- **Alpha**: This measures the weight given to the data points. A higher value means that we are giving a higher weight to recent data points.
- **Beta**: This measures the weight given to the trend. A higher value means that we are giving a higher weight to the recent trend.
- **Gamma**: This measures the weight given to the season. A higher value means that we are giving a higher weight to the recent seasonal period.
- **Mean Absolute Scaled Error (MASE)**: This measures the accuracy of the forecasts.
- **Symmetric Mean Absolute Percentage Error (SMAPE)**: This measures the accuracy based on percentage errors.
- **Mean Absolute Percentage Error (AE)**: This measures the accuracy based on percentage errors.
- **Root Mean Squared Error (RMSE)**: This measures the differences between predicted and observed values.

We have explained how to use Excel's built-in capabilities to analyze and forecast time series. In the next section, we will focus on the importance of time series stationarity.

# Studying the stationarity of a time series

Most methods for a time series forecast rely on the fact that the series is stationary. This makes sense, since this increases the probability of repeating a certain behavior in the future and makes the prediction easier.

How can we know whether a given time series is stationary or not? There are formal, statistical methods to measure this, but we can also look at some properties of the series. There are three main checks of stationarity in practice:

- The mean value is constant (does not depend on time).
- The variance is constant.
- The covariance of the elements $i$ and $i+m$ is constant.

In our previous example, in the *Modeling and visualizing time series* section, we plotted the moving average (mean) and variance. If you revisit the diagram, you will see that none of them is constant with time, hence the series is non-stationary, and we had to model it to be able to forecast values.

A more formal statistical test is the *Dickey-Fuller test*, which is out of the scope of this book. This test is not automatically done by Excel, but there are a large number of add-ins that can perform it. Doing it manually makes no sense.

There are two ways of removing seasonality and trend:

- The technique of decomposing the series into noise, periodic, and increasing terms.
- Differencing – that is, creating a new series by taking the difference between the values $i$ and $(i+m)$. The position difference, $m$ is known as **lag**.

You have now seen different methods for predicting the evolution of a time series, based on a detailed understanding of its characteristics. We will show more advanced forecasting methods, such as ARIMA, when we discuss using Azure machine learning models from Excel in Chapter 10, *Azure and Excel – Machine Learning in the Cloud*.

Visualization was also a key element throughout the analysis shown in the present chapter. We will see different visualization techniques in the next chapter, focusing in their particular use cases.

# Summary

We have seen a step-by-step method to decompose a time series and forecast its future values. This can help us, at least in general terms, to predict the outcome of different processes. Time series can be studied both graphically and numerically, extracting their characteristics and using them to understand how they will behave in the future. We have also seen that this can be done automatically in Excel, with the risk of using it as a black box and not understanding the full forecasting method. More advanced techniques exist, and we will discuss them in future chapters.

The next chapter will show you how to build some basic diagrams in Excel and how to use them to gain insights on your datasets.

# Questions

1. In our forecast, we modeled the increasing part of the time series using the trend function generated by Excel. We could also have used the moving average values. How can that be done? Try it and compare the results.
2. Change the values of the seasonality and confidence interval and study how the forecast diagram and parameters change.
3. How can you calculate the covariance between two values in a time series?
4. A possible way to make the variance independent of time is to take the logarithm of the time series values. Try this in the air passengers series and check the values of the variance.

# Further reading

- *Time Series Analysis and Its Applications*, by R.H. Shumway and D.S. Stoffer
- *An Introductory Study on Time Series Modeling and Forecasting*, by Ratnadip Adhikari R. K. Agrawal

# 4
# Section 4: Data Visualization and Advanced Machine Learning

There are many types of visualizations that are well known and that provide important information about our datasets and results. Each type of data and analysis has its own corresponding visualization.

Many data analysis and machine learning projects never pass the proof-of-concept stage. It is important to get them to a production environment where the analysis is continuous, from data extraction through to visualization.

This section comprises the following chapters:

- Chapter 8, *Visualizing Data in Diagrams, Histograms, and Maps*
- Chapter 9, *Artificial Neural Networks*
- Chapter 10, *Azure and Excel - Machine Learning in the Cloud*
- Chapter 11, *The Future of Machine Learning*

# 8
# Visualizing Data in Diagrams, Histograms, and Maps

If we are talking about machine learning, why should we care about visualization? The answer is simple: if you cannot show what you have analyzed and the outcome of your models to somebody without any technical knowledge, then you will not be able to show any added value. We have already shown how important data visualization is for understanding a dataset and to decide which features will be most useful for training our model. We are now going to investigate which type of diagram is best suited to tell the story of our data and the new information we got from it.

The following topics will be covered in this chapter:

- Showing basic comparisons and relationships between variables
- Building data distributions using histograms
- Representing geographical distribution of data in maps
- Showing data that changes over time

## Technical requirements

To complete this chapter, the reader will need to download the `1976USpresident.xlsx` and `subte.xlsx` files from the GitHub repository at `https://github.com/PacktPublishing/Hands-On-Machine-Learning-with-Microsoft-Excel-2019/tree/master/Chapter08`.

# Showing basic comparisons and relationships between variables

Data visualization is extremely important in the context of data analytics and machine learning. Some of the reasons for this are as follows:

- Tell the story of your data and help decision makers with their job.
- Predict the future evolution of some variable(s).
- Find hidden trends and patterns in the data.
- Find outliers, that is, anomalies in the data.
- Understand the distribution, composition, and relationships.
- Build groups and categories.

We will show different types of charts used to show different types of data. The data used in the example charts is as follows:

| Year | Sales | Cost | Profit | ROI |
|------|-------|------|--------|-----|
| 2015 | 23455 | 18294.9 | 5160.1 | 28.21% |
| 2016 | 19226 | 12881.42 | 6344.58 | 49.25% |
| 2017 | 34557 | 24881.04 | 9675.96 | 38.89% |
| 2018 | 20134 | 14697.82 | 5436.18 | 36.99% |
| 2019 | 22314 | 14057.82 | 8256.18 | 58.73% |

Also consider the following data:

| Year | SalesA | CostA | ProfitA | SalesB | CostB | ProfitB |
|------|--------|-------|---------|--------|-------|---------|
| 2015 | 23455 | 18294.9 | 5160.1 | 23455 | 18294.9 | 5160.1 |
| 2016 | 19226 | 12881.42 | 6344.58 | 19226 | 12881.42 | 6344.58 |
| 2017 | 34557 | 24881.04 | 9675.96 | 34557 | 24881.04 | 9675.96 |
| 2018 | 20134 | 14697.82 | 5436.18 | 20134 | 14697.82 | 5436.18 |
| 2019 | 22314 | 14057.82 | 8256.18 | 22314 | 14057.82 | 8256.18 |

Type this data into an Excel worksheet so that you can create the charts shown in the following sections.

# The basic parts of an Excel diagram

An Excel chart has different parts and it is important to know their names so that we can modify the chart at will. The following chart shows them in detail:

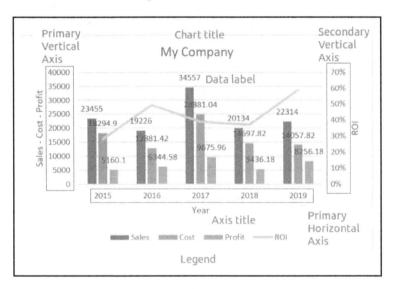

The *x* axis represents the data categories and the *y* axis the data series.

 All charts shown in the following subsections can be created by selecting the data range and navigating to **Insert | Recommended Charts**. There, we see previews and select the one that better tells the story of our data.

# Column charts

Clustered column charts can be used when you want to show between two and four different data series in the same chart. To plot only one series does not make sense, and more than four might look cluttered. Look at the following example:

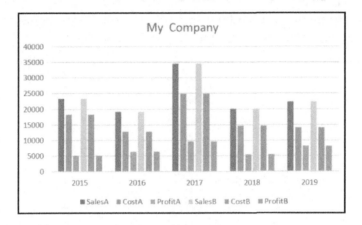

In this case, it certainly looks better if we split the data, for example, to show a smaller group of years and to switch the time series and categories (see the following chart):

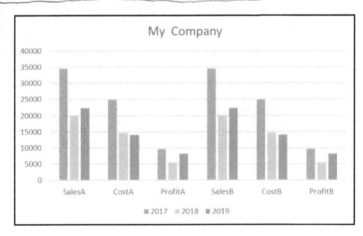

The series in the column charts should be expressed in the same units, otherwise they cannot be compared, or their comparison might be misguiding.

# Combination charts

If we need to show data series expressed in different units, we can use combination charts. The basic difference is that these charts have two vertical axes with different units of measurement. The following chart shows an example of this:

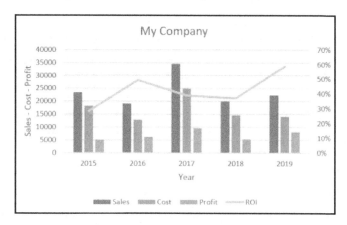

In this case, the primary vertical axis (left) is expressed in currency units and the secondary vertical axis in percentages.

# Stacked charts

This type of chart is used when it is important to point out the importance of the relative values in the data series. For example, *Cost + Profit = Sales*. We can see that it is easy to compare the values at first sight, as in the following chart:

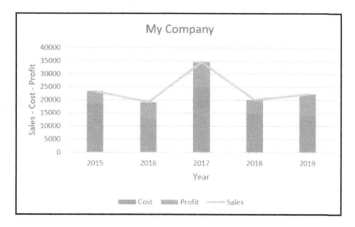

This chart can be created by first including the **Cost** and **Profit** variables and then adding **Sales**.

# Pie and bar charts

A pie chart is useful to compare many series. As an example we will use the results of the 2016 US President Election in the state of Oregon, listed in the following table:

| Candidate | Votes |
|---|---:|
| Clinton, Hillary | 1,002,106 |
| Trump, Donald J. | 782,403 |
| Johnson, Gary | 94,231 |
| Other | 72,594 |
| Stein, Jill | 50,002 |

The resulting pie chart is as follows:

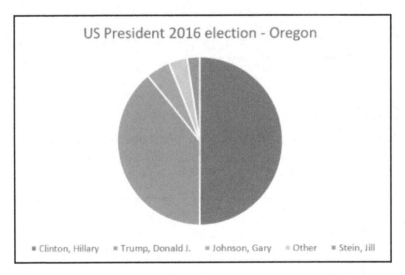

The same results can be shown in a bar chart, and the differences in the number of votes are easier to compare.

Change the chart type to a bar chart by right-clicking on any part of the diagram.

The bar chart will look similar to the following:

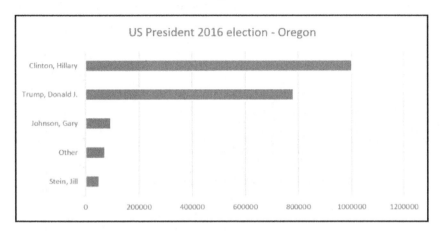

We know now how to choose the best diagrams for each type of data. In the following section, we will study one of the most important and most often used diagrams when previewing data using histograms.

# Building data distributions using histograms

We used histograms in Chapter 5, *Correlations and the Importance of Variables*, without formally introducing them. This type of chart shows the count of values, either numerical or categorical. To show numerical data, we can build categories, as we did with the age of the Titanic passengers:

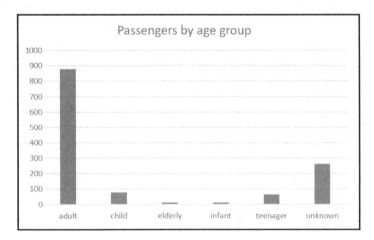

Or, we could have used the age variable as a number and distributed the values in bins (groups of data points falling between the same numerical range):

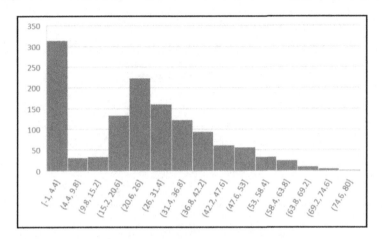

The preceding histogram was created following these steps:

1. Navigate to **Insert** | **Histogram.**
2. Double-click the *x* axis to set the number of bins to 15.

We can immediately see a large amount of entries in the first bin corresponding to the missing age values, which we defined as -1 to identify them easily. We also notice that the larger number of passengers were between 20 and 26 years old and that the distribution is not symmetrical; it seems to show an exponential decay toward older ages and a much faster decrease in younger ones. This can be interpreted by thinking about the fact that not many small children travelled in a transatlantic ship (at least at the time of the Titanic sinking).

You will also notice that histograms are an excellent graphical method for spotting **outliers**; that is, data points that do not follow the same distribution as the rest. In our current example, missing values are also outliers.

Another useful application of histograms is in comparing values when there are a large number of items to compare. Let's suppose that we made a prediction using a machine learning model. We are predicting a numerical value and we want to compare it with the real one to test our model. We can then, for each set of feature values, plot the difference between the real and predicted values. If our model is a good predictor, we should see something like the following chart:

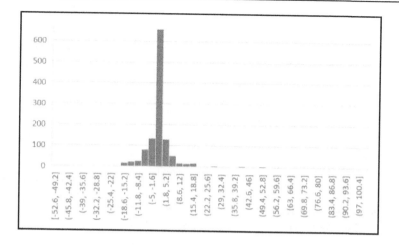

The distribution is centered at **0** and is mostly symmetrical, with a few large values toward the right. These are, obviously, bad predictions.

We have seen that histograms are a valuable tool for identifying different characteristics of the datasets. Let's concentrate now on more complex data representations.

# Representing geographical distribution of data in maps

Localizing information in a map is extremely useful to understand data in the spatial dimension, which is often difficult by other means. Excel offers different options and we are going to show a couple of them. We will start by using data containing geographical coordinates, that is, latitude and longitude. The widespread use of the GPS system nowadays makes it easy to obtain this information. In any case, if this precise information is not available, we will see that the built-in information in Excel will still make it simple to draw maps and show us useful information.

In our first example, we will use data from the *Massachusetts Institute of Technology Election Data and Science Lab* about the 1976 US presidential election. The `1976USpresident.xlsx` file contains, among other information, the list of US states and the vote count for each presidential candidate. We would like to put this information in a map, resembling those shown in the news with Republican states colored in red and Democrat states colored in blue.

The input data table is the following:

From this table, we need to extract the winner party in each state, namely the one with more votes. We will use **Power Query** and its **Group By** function.

1. Navigate to **Data | From Table/Range**.
2. Open the **Power Query** window. You should see something similar to the following screenshot:

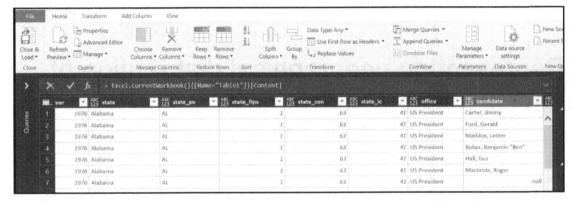

3. Select **Group By | Advanced** then select **state** for the **Group by** option.
4. Then, we will add a new column called `Winner`, where we will **Sum** the values of **party**. This will give an error, but will give us the base function to get the winner party name later.
5. The second column we will add is named `Votes`, where we select the maximum value of **candidatevotes**. This will show the larger number of votes in each state.

The following screenshot shows how the window should look like after selecting the detailed options:

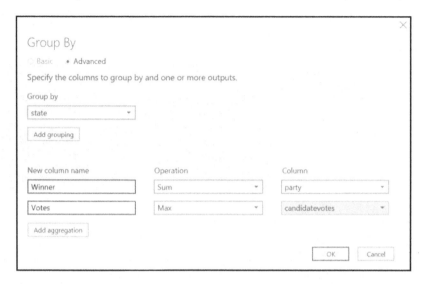

After clicking **OK**, the resulting table is as follows:

6. To fix the error and get the party name in the `Winner` column, we replace the function:

   = *Table.Group(#"Changed Type", {"state"}, {{"Winner", each List.**Sum**([party]), type text}, {"Votes", each List.Max([candidatevotes]), type number}})*

We replace the preceding function with the following:

   = *Table.Group(#"Changed Type", {"state"}, {{"Winner", each List.**First**([party]), type text}, {"Votes", each List.Max([candidatevotes]), type number}})*

This will show the winning party, like in the following table:

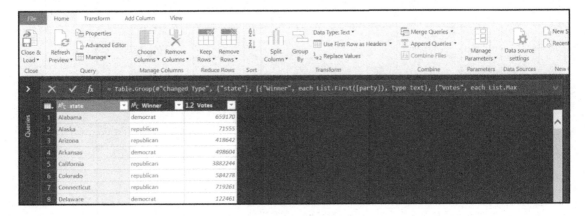

7. Click on **Close & Load**.
8. Use the generated table to create the map. Select any cell in the table and then navigate to **Insert | Recommended Charts**. The first suggestion will be a map like the one we want.
9. Click **OK**.
10. Change the title and colors by double-clicking on the legends. The resulting map is as follows:

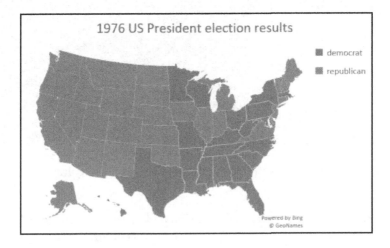

Our second example will use data from the Argentinean Government public database (datos.gob.ar). The latitude and longitude of all underground stations in Buenos Aires is listed, together with their names and the lines they belong to.

The nickname of the Buenos Aires underground is **Subte**, a short form of the word **subterráneo (underground)**, hence the name of the file.

Geographical coordinates are not accepted as input in regular Excel maps, so we are going to show the 3D Maps functions, which also has other advantages.

Perform the following steps:

1. Load the `subte.xlsx` file and you will see the following table (partially shown):

2. Select the full data range.
3. Navigate to **Insert | 3D Map**. You should see something similar to the following screenshot:

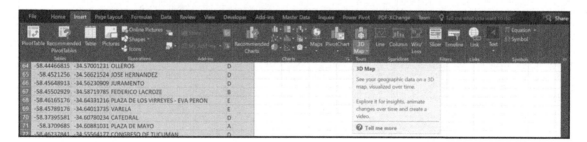

Should the icon be greyed out, refer link `https://support.office.com/en-ie/article/get-started-with-3d-maps-6b56a50d-3c3e-4a9e-a527-eea62a387030` for step-by-step instructions to activate 3D Maps.

4. Click on **New tour** as shown in the following screenshot:

The 3D Maps window will open, showing the default view of Earth, as seen in the following screenshot:

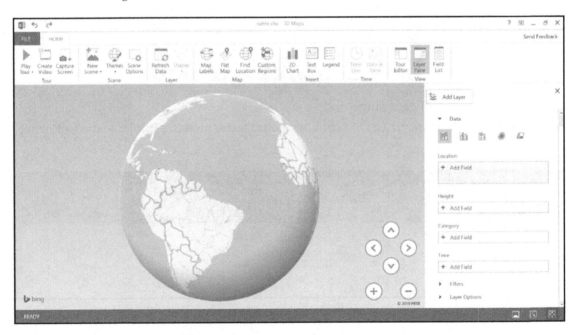

5. Add two fields to the **Location** window: Long and Lat. They should be automatically assigned to the corresponding variables. If not, select them from the menu to the right of the names (see the following screenshot).

6. The map should now be centered in the city of Buenos Aires, but the zoom might still be too far out.

7. Zoom in by scrolling with your mouse or using the **+** button.

8. In the **Category** field, add **Line**, since we want to distinguish between the different groups of stations.

9. The map will look similar to this screenshot:

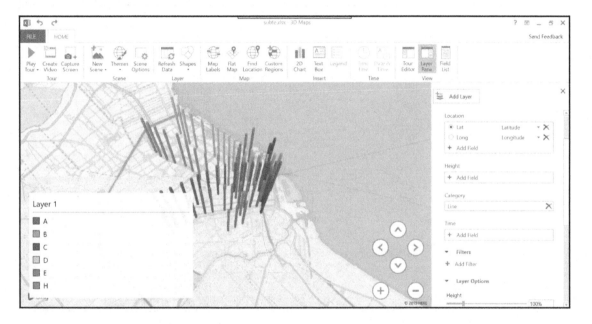

Let's improve it a little. Instead of those large columns representing each station, we want small symbols. To achieve this, perform the following steps:

1. Click on **Layer Options.**
2. Set **Height** to **0%** and **Thickness** to between **50%** and **70%**.
3. You can also change the color for each line (category). As in many other cities, the Subte lines are identified by colors. **A** is light blue, **B** is red, **C** is blue, **D** is green, **E** is purple, and **H** is yellow (what happened to **F** and **G**? They, and **I**, are not yet built). The final result is shown in the following screenshot:

One last thing we can do, since 3D Maps can be used interactively, is to add useful information to the data card (or tool tip, as it is usually called in visualizations). To do this, perform the following steps:

1. Click on the **Customize** button (below **Data Card**) and you can see that, by default, the three variables included so far are there (see the following sample screenshot):

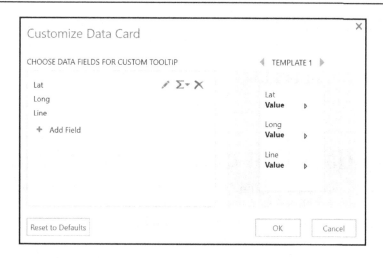

2. Delete **Lat** and **Long** by clicking on the red X.
3. Add **Station**.

After this, if we move the mouse over any of the symbols representing the underground stations, we will see its name and the line it belongs to, like in the following screenshot:

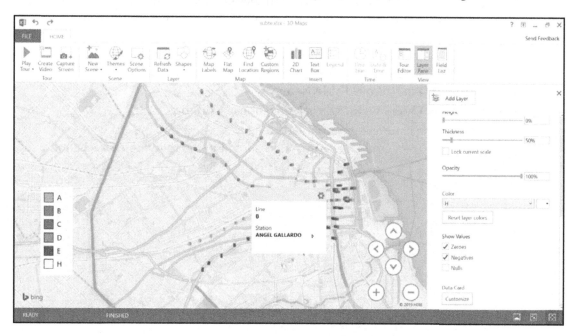

We now know how to use Excel to usefully represent geographical data, using both the names of places or GPS coordinates.

In our last example, we will revisit time series to show the different ways of representing them.

# Showing data that changes over time

In previous chapters, we analyzed time series in detail. We mainly used line charts to represent the evolution of the data. Can time evolution be represented in a different way? We know from experience that lines can be misguiding when we want to compare two values, and that other methods are better.

Going back to the US election data, suppose we want to compare the time evolution of the two major parties, Democrat and Republican, in one state, over several years. Perform the following steps:

1.  Load the `1976_2016USpresident.xlsx` file in Excel and you will see the same information in the table that we used in the previous section, except that we can now see the results corresponding to every election in every state from 1976 to 2016.
2.  Select one state at random (California, in our case) and try to compare how the number of votes per party changed with time.
3.  Navigate to **Data | From Table/Range**.
4.  In the **Power Query** window, click on **Choose Columns**.
5.  Select only the columns we are interested in: `year`, `state`, `party`, `candidatevotes`, and `totalvotes`, as shown in the following screenshot:

6. Add a new column by clicking on **Add Column | Custom Column** to calculate the percentage of votes by party, that is, *[candidatevotes]/[totalvotes]*.

7. Change the type of that column to **Percentage** (in **Home | Data Type**). The result is similar to what is shown in the following screenshot:

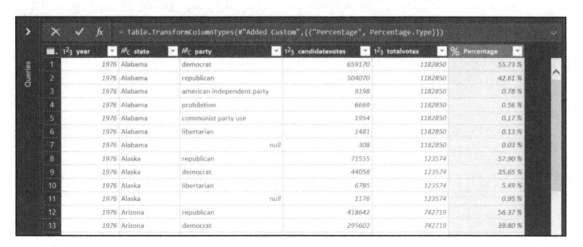

8. Filter the rows to leave only `state` as `California` and `party` as `republican` or `democrat`.

We need to format the table in such a way that we can compare both time series in a meaningful way. To do this, perform the following steps:

1. Select the `party` column.
2. Navigate to **Transform.**
3. Click on **Pivot Column**. The pop-up window should look like the following screenshot before clicking **OK**:

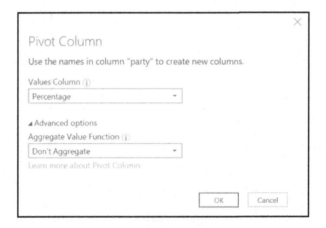

The result is the following table:

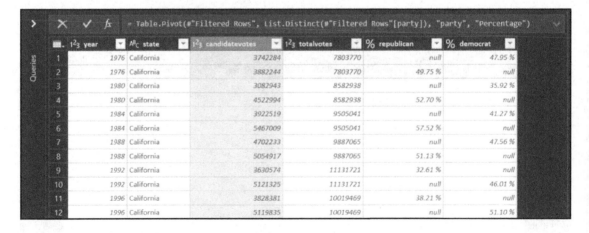

| | 1²₃ year | ᴬᴮc state | 1²₃ candidatevotes | 1²₃ totalvotes | % republican | % democrat |
|---|---|---|---|---|---|---|
| 1 | 1976 | California | 3742284 | 7803770 | null | 47.95 % |
| 2 | 1976 | California | 3882244 | 7803770 | 49.75 % | null |
| 3 | 1980 | California | 3082943 | 8582938 | null | 35.92 % |
| 4 | 1980 | California | 4522994 | 8582938 | 52.70 % | null |
| 5 | 1984 | California | 3922519 | 9505041 | null | 41.27 % |
| 6 | 1984 | California | 5467009 | 9505041 | 57.52 % | null |
| 7 | 1988 | California | 4702233 | 9887065 | null | 47.56 % |
| 8 | 1988 | California | 5054917 | 9887065 | 51.13 % | null |
| 9 | 1992 | California | 3630574 | 11131721 | 32.61 % | null |
| 10 | 1992 | California | 5121325 | 11131721 | null | 46.01 % |
| 11 | 1996 | California | 3828381 | 10019469 | 38.21 % | null |
| 12 | 1996 | California | 5119835 | 10019469 | null | 51.10 % |

We will now repeat some steps that we have used before, so I will explain them quickly:

1. Select both % columns.
2. Navigate to **Transform | Replace Values.**
3. Change all `nulls` to zeroes.
4. Use **Home | Group By** to group by state.
5. Select **Sum** as aggregation.
6. The last step would be to create another column to account for the difference between the percentage of Democrat and Republican votes and the total:

   *100%- % republican -% democrat*

This will give us the percentage of votes going to other parties. The table we will use to create the diagram is as follows:

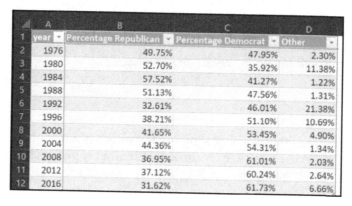

| | A | B | C | D |
|---|---|---|---|---|
| 1 | year | Percentage Republican | Percentage Democrat | Other |
| 2 | 1976 | 49.75% | 47.95% | 2.30% |
| 3 | 1980 | 52.70% | 35.92% | 11.38% |
| 4 | 1984 | 57.52% | 41.27% | 1.22% |
| 5 | 1988 | 51.13% | 47.56% | 1.31% |
| 6 | 1992 | 32.61% | 46.01% | 21.38% |
| 7 | 1996 | 38.21% | 51.10% | 10.69% |
| 8 | 2000 | 41.65% | 53.45% | 4.90% |
| 9 | 2004 | 44.36% | 54.31% | 1.34% |
| 10 | 2008 | 36.95% | 61.01% | 2.03% |
| 11 | 2012 | 37.12% | 60.24% | 2.64% |
| 12 | 2016 | 31.62% | 61.73% | 6.66% |

7. Click on any cell in the chart.
8. Navigate to **Insert | Recommended Charts.**
9. Choose **Stacked Bars.**

The result will be something similar to the following diagram:

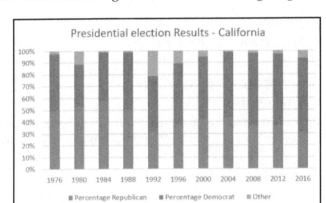

It is clear that this type of chart is better for comparing the amount of votes obtained by each party and other details of the data. For example, we immediately see that, in 1992, both parties, but especially Republican, lost votes to other, non-traditional parties.

 Hint: search for `Ross Perot` in Google.

We have shown there are other ways of showing the information contained in a time series beyond the line charts. You can now experiment with other types of charts, depending on the information you need to display.

# Summary

We have discussed different types of diagrams in Excel, which can be used to compare variables and show data in meaningful ways, helping us to extract value from our results.

We can now go back to the pure machine learning models and take a leap forward to the advanced world of neural networks.

# Questions

1. What types of data can be represented in charts? Make a list and think about the best charts to use in each case.
2. What happens when you try to use a pie chart to show more than five or six data series?
3. What type of chart would be a good alternative to stacked bars?
4. Try using other geographical data (for example, street addresses) to create a diagram.
5. Can you use the US President election data to predict the results for 2020? In principle, it should be possible to forecast the values of the time series. Try it and think about the accuracy of the predictions and the possible explanations.

# Further reading

- *The Visual Display of Quantitative Information*, by Edward R.Tufte
- *Storytelling with Data: A Data Visualization Guide for Business Professionals*, by Cole Nussbaumer Knaflic

# 9
# Artificial Neural Networks

Artificial neural networks try to mimic the way the human brain works. They are used to solve a number of difficult problems, such as understanding written or spoken language, identifying objects in an image, or driving a car.

You will learn the basics of how an artificial neural network works, look at the steps and mathematical calculations needed to train it, and have a general view of complex neural networks.

The following topics will be covered in this chapter:

- Introducing the perceptron – the simplest type of neural network
- Building a deep network
- Understanding the backpropagation algorithm

# Technical requirements

To complete this chapter, you will need to download the transfusion.xlsx file from the GitHub repository at https://github.com/PacktPublishing/Hands-On-Machine-Learning-with-Microsoft-Excel-2019/tree/master/Chapter09.

# Introducing the perceptron – the simplest type of neural network

Neural networks are inspired by the human brain' more specifically, by the neuron cells that compose it. Actually, since there have been major advances in neuroscience since the first artificial neuron was designed, it would be better to say that they are inspired by what was known about the brain some years ago.

The perceptron was the first attempt to build an artificial neural network (Frank Rosenblatt, 1959). It was actually a model of a single neuron, with multiple inputs and one output. The value at the output is calculated as the weighted sum of the inputs and these weights are adjusted iteratively. This simple implementation has many disadvantages and limitations, so it was later replaced by the multilayer perceptron. The most basic model of this artificial neural network has the structure shown in the following diagram:

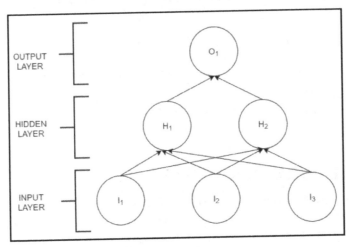

The input and output layers are taken from the perceptron, but a hidden layer of nodes is now added. Each node in this layer acts in practice as a neuron. To understand how the inputs and outputs of each neuron work and how information is sent through the network, we need to know the details of how each neuron is built. A schematic view of an artificial neuron could be represented as follows:

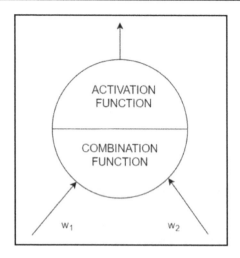

The combination function calculates the resulting input as the sum of the inputs weighted by $w_i$. The activation function calculates the output using this input. The output range is usually limited to [0;1], using different functions. It is often the case that the neuron transmits the signal only if the input value is above a certain threshold.

How does an artificial neural network learn? A training dataset is used, for which the outputs are known. The input values are fed into the network, the predicted output is compared to the real output, and the $w_i$ weights are adjusted iteratively at each step. This means that a neural network is a supervised learning model.

The more complex the problem, the larger the number of training samples needed to adjust the weights. We will also see that the number of hidden layers and neurons are also adjusted depending on the problem. Fine tuning these parameters is a complex problem, almost a field of study in itself.

Artificial neural networks are useful since they can model any mathematical function. So, even if the relationship between the input values is unknown, we can use a network to reproduce it and make predictions.

Since the training process can be complicated and the number of parameters that are adjusted at training time is large, it is often difficult to understand why an artificial neural network correctly predicts a given value. The explainability of the artificial intelligence models, based on neural networks, is also an extensively studied problem.

Some applications of neural networks are as follows:

- Image analysis—faces, objects, colors, expressions, and gestures
- Sound analysis—voices, speech to text, and sentiment
- Text classification—email spam, fraud in document content, and sentiment
- Hardware failures—predictive and/or diagnostic
- Health risks and/or diagnostics
- Customer or employee churn

Let's see how training works in practice, following an example.

# Training a neural network

We will use a public dataset from the Blood Transfusion Service Center in Hsin-Chu City, Taiwan (*Knowledge discovery on RFM model using Bernoulli sequence*, by Yeh, I-Cheng, Yang, King-Jang, and Ting, Tao-Ming, Expert Systems with Applications, 2008). The set contains information about blood donors, summarized in five variables:

- R (Recency – months since last donation)
- F (Frequency – total number of donations)
- M (Monetary – total blood donated in c.c.)
- T (Time – months since first donation)
- A binary variable representing whether they donated blood in March 2007 (one stands for donating blood; zero stands for not donating blood)

We would like to prove how well an artificial neural network can learn from the first four of the preceding features, and predict the target, variable five. Follow these steps to reproduce and learn about the calculations already shown in the transfusion.xlsx file:

1. Load the transfusion.xlsx file into Excel.

2. In the worksheet named `transfusion`, you will find the input data. It should look something like the following screenshot:

| | A | B | C | D | E | F |
|---|---|---|---|---|---|---|
| 1 | Recency (months) | Frequency (times) | Monetary (c.c. blood) | Time (months) | whether he/she donated blood in March 2007 | |
| 2 | 2 | 50 | 12500 | 98 | | 1 |
| 3 | 0 | 13 | 3250 | 28 | | 1 |
| 4 | 1 | 16 | 4000 | 35 | | 1 |
| 5 | 2 | 20 | 5000 | 45 | | 1 |
| 6 | 1 | 24 | 6000 | 77 | | 0 |
| 7 | 4 | 4 | 1000 | 4 | | 0 |
| 8 | 2 | 7 | 1750 | 14 | | 1 |
| 9 | 1 | 12 | 3000 | 35 | | 0 |
| 10 | 2 | 9 | 2250 | 22 | | 1 |
| 11 | 5 | 46 | 11500 | 98 | | 1 |
| 12 | 4 | 23 | 5750 | 58 | | 0 |
| 13 | 0 | 3 | 750 | 4 | | 0 |
| 14 | 2 | 10 | 2500 | 28 | | 1 |
| 15 | 1 | 13 | 3250 | 47 | | 0 |
| 16 | 2 | 6 | 1500 | 15 | | 1 |
| 17 | 2 | 5 | 1250 | 11 | | 1 |
| 18 | 2 | 14 | 3500 | 48 | | 1 |
| 19 | 2 | 15 | 3750 | 49 | | 1 |
| 20 | 2 | 6 | 1500 | 15 | | 1 |
| 21 | 2 | 3 | 750 | 4 | | 1 |
| 22 | 2 | 3 | 750 | 4 | | 1 |
| 23 | 4 | 11 | 2750 | 28 | | 0 |
| 24 | 2 | 6 | 1500 | 16 | | 1 |
| 25 | 2 | 6 | 1500 | 16 | | 1 |

*(handwritten annotations: INPUT 1, INPUT 2, INPUT 3, INPUT 4, TARGET; X1, X2, X3, X4, Y)*

Reference | transfusion | training | test | ⊕

3. Since the data is not presented in any particular order, we can use the first 500 entries to train the neural network. Open a new worksheet and rename it `training1` (remember that we are repeating the steps to create the worksheets already present in the file, so that you can compare your results).

4. Create a set of variables like the one you see in the following screenshot. If you use the same cells, it will be easier to follow the next steps:

| | A | B | C | D | E | F | G | H | I | J | K | L | M | N | O |
|---|---|---|---|---|---|---|---|---|---|---|---|---|---|---|---|
| 1 | Neural network with 4 inputs, one hidden layer with 2 neurons | | | | | | | | | | | | | | |
| 2 | | | | | | | | | | | | | | | |
| 3 | | | | w11 | | | | | | | | | | | |
| 4 | | | | w12 | | | | | | | | | | | |
| 5 | | | | w13 | | | | | | | | | | | |
| 6 | | | | w14 | | | | | | | | | | | |
| 7 | | | | w21 | | | | | | | | | | | |
| 8 | | | | w22 | | | | | | | | | | | |
| 9 | | | | w23 | | | | | | | | | | | |
| 10 | | | | w24 | | | | | | | | | | | |
| 11 | | | | theta0 | | | | | | | | | | | |
| 12 | | | | theta1 | | | | | | | | | | | |
| 13 | | | | theta2 | | | | | | | | | | | |
| 14 | | | | | | | | | | | | | | | |
| 15 | | | | Sq error | | | | | | | | | | | |
| 16 | | | | | | | | | | | | | | | |
| 17 | | | | | | | | | | | | | | | |
| 18 | | | | | | | | | | | | | | | |
| 19 | Train data | | | | | | | | | | | | | | |
| 20 | | | | | | | | | | | | | | | |
| 21 | # | x1 | x2 | x3 | x4 | y | | wsum1 | wsum2 | at1 | at2 | Output | Error | Sq error | round_out |
| 22 | | | | | | | | | | | | | | | |
| 23 | | | | | | | | | | | | | | | |

If we build an artificial neural network with four inputs (the four features in the input data) and one hidden layer containing two neurons, we need eight weight parameters: $w_{11}$, $w_{12}$, $w_{13}$, and $w_{14}$ for hidden neuron one, and $w_{21}$, $w_{21}$, $w_{23}$ and $w_{24}$ for hidden neuron two. The remaining parameters will be explained later.

5. From the worksheet named `transfusion`, copy the first 500 data rows (excluding the header).
6. In the `training1` worksheet click on cell *B22*.
7. Paste the copied cells.
8. You now have a table containing the input values, called $x_1$, $x_2$, $x_3$ and $x_4$, plus the output binary value, y. Column # in the table just shows the row number.

The combination function of the hidden neuron *j* is the weighted sum of the inputs, as shown in the following formula:

$$wsumj = \sum_{i=1}^{N} w_{ji} \cdot x_i$$

*[handwritten top margin: MINIMAL WEIGHTS ; INPUTS V WEIGHTS (2 NEU.)]*

In our example, N=4, which gives us the next two expressions:

$$wsum1 = w_{11}.x_1 + w_{12}.x_2 + w_{13}.x_3 + w_{14}.x_4$$

$$wsum2 = w_{21}.x_1 + w_{22}.x_2 + w_{23}.x_3 + w_{24}.x_4$$

9. Taking into account these expressions, write the following formula in cell G22:

=$E$3*B22+$E$4*C22+$E$5*D22+$E$6*E22

In cell H22, write the following:

=$E$7*B22+$E$8*C22+$E$9*D22+$E$10*E22

10. Copy these expressions down to the rest of the cells in columns G and H. The simplest and most commonly used activation function is the following sigmoid function:

$$s(x) = \frac{1}{1 + e^{-x}}$$

In our example, x is the combination function calculated for each hidden neuron and each entry used for training:

$$s1 = s(wsum1) = \frac{1}{1 + e^{-wsum1}}$$

$$s2 = s(wsum2) = \frac{1}{1 + e^{-wsum2}}$$

11. Define cell I22 as =1/(1+EXP(-G22)) and cell J22 as =1/(1+EXP(-H22)).

12. Copy these formulas down to the rest of the rows in columns I and J. The last calculation is the neural network output, which is a weighted sum of the outputs from the hidden neurons, plus a constant value that acts as a threshold; if the total input is less that this value, the output is zero and the network does not activate. This can be expressed by the following formula:

$$Output = \theta_0 + \theta_1.s1 + \theta_2.s2$$

*[handwritten: → threshold]*

*[handwritten left: $PUT = \theta + \sum \theta_j \cdot S_j$]*

*[handwritten right: OPTIMIZED WEIGHTS = IF TOTAL INPUT < OUTPUT]*

*[handwritten annotations:
$w_1 - \sum_1 w_1$
$w_2 - \sum_2 w_2$
$w_3 - \sum_3 w_3$
$w_4 - \sum_4 w_4$
$w_5 - \sum_5 w_5$
$w_6 - \sum_3 w_6$
$w_7 - \sum_3 w_7$
$w_8 - \sum_4 w_8$
$\sum w_{ij} \cdot x_i$
$\theta = output - \sum w \cdot x$
$\theta_0 = output$]*

*[handwritten bottom: $\frac{1}{1 + \frac{1}{e^x}} = \frac{1}{\frac{e^x+1}{e^x}} = \frac{e^x}{e^x+1}$]*

13. You can then write the following in cell *K22*:

$$=\$E\$11+\$E\$12*I22+\$E\$13*J22$$

14. Copy the formula down to the rest of the cells in column K. Since *E11*, *E12*, and *E13* are the cells we have saved for theta 1, theta 2 and theta 3 respectively. We use all the defined weights and parameters in our calculations, but we don't have values for them. Training a neural network implies finding the values for these parameters that make the output as close as the target value as possible, for example, for each combination of $x_1$, $x_2$, $x_3$, and $x_4$, the difference between the value of *Output* and the value of $y$ should be the minimum possible. We need to calculate three values then: the output error (Output-y), the squared error (Error²), and the sum of the squared errors, which is the value to minimize.

> **TIP**
>
> The function we are minimizing, the sum of the squared errors, is only one possible **loss function**. There are other functions that are used to compare the output of the neural network with the training value. Studying when to apply each function is shown in more advanced machine learning books.

15. Define cell L22 as =*K22-F22*.
16. Copy the formula down to the rest of the rows in column L.
17. Define cell M22 as =*L22^2*.
18. Copy the formula down to the rest of the rows in column M.
19. Define cell E15 as =*SUM(M22:M521)*. This is the sum of the squared errors.

We can now use Excel's Solver to set values to $w_{11}$, $w_{12}$, $w_{13}$, $w_{14}$, $w_{21}$, $w_{21}$, $w_{23}$, $w_{24}$, $\theta_o$, $\theta_1$, and $\theta_2$, while minimizing the sum of the squared errors:

1. Navigate to **Data.**
2. Click on **Solver.**

3. Fill in the details as shown in the following screenshot:

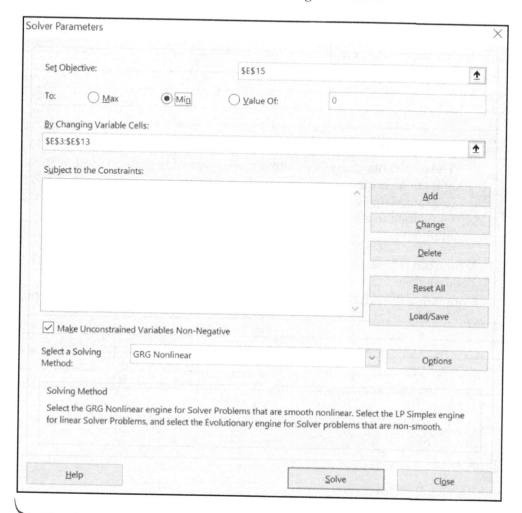

The objective is E15, where we store the sum of squared errors, and the variable cells E3 to E13.

4. Click on **Solve.**

5. The optimal result is shown in the following table:

| Parameters | Values |
| --- | --- |
| w11 | -3.915205816 |
| w12 | 0.055009315 |
| w13 | 0.016855755 |

| w14 | -0.301397506 |
|---|---|
| w21 | -0.016701972 |
| w22 | 0.451221978 |
| w23 | -0.001645853 |
| w24 | -0.011395209 |
| theta0 | -0.349977457 |
| theta1 | 0.247932886 |
| theta2 | 1.256803829 |
| **Square error** | **77.02669809** |

The results may vary depending on the type of regression used in Solver and on the initial values. The gradient descent algorithm search (explained in the *Understanding the backpropagation algorithm* section) might be trapped in a local minimum that has a larger value than the global minimum.

6. Define cell N22 as *=round(K22)* to convert the output of the neural network to binary values.

7. Comparing the predicted and linear values, you can build the confusion matrix:

|  |  | Real |  |
|---|---|---|---|
|  |  | 1 | 0 |
| Predicted | 1 | 32 | 22 |
|  | 0 | 86 | 360 |

Use the confusion matrix to measure the accuracy of the neural network training.

# Testing the neural network

Once you are satisfied with the training, you can use the values obtained for the parameters to **predict** the y value for the rest of the data (which was never used in the training, and can then be used to test the network output).

Follow these steps to predict the target variable using the test dataset:

1. Make a copy of the worksheet named `training1`. Name the new worksheet `test1`.
2. Delete the range of cells *B22:F521*.
3. Copy the last 248 rows in the worksheet named `transfusion` to the new worksheet, starting on cell B22.
4. All calculations should work and you should be able to see the results of using the test data as input.

We have now developed a simple exercise that shows how an artificial neural network learns from input data. The calculations we made are the base of the **backpropagation** algorithm, which is explained in detail in the last section of this chapter.

# Building a deep network

Our example of artificial neural network is very simple and only contains one hidden layer. Can we add more layers? Of course we can! The next step in complexity could be something similar to the following diagram:

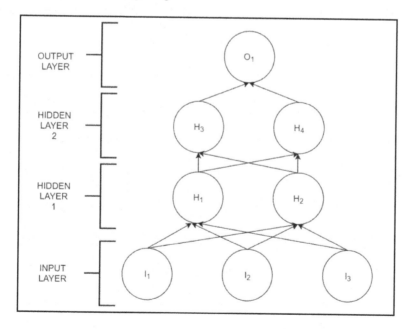

We added a new hidden layer with two neurons, but we could add more layers and more neurons per layer. The architecture of a network depends on the specific use we give it. Multilayer artificial neural networks are often known as **deep neural networks**.

The output of a deep network is calculated in analogy with the single layer one, considering all inputs to each neuron, the activation function, and the addition of all the inputs to the output neuron. Looking at the preceding diagram, it is clear that each layer in the network is affected by the previous one. It is usually the case that, in order to solve complex problems, each layer learns a specific set of characteristics. For example, when identifying an image, the first layer could train on colors, the second on shapes, the third on objects, and so on, increasing in complexity as we advance toward the output.

As we add more neurons to the network, there are more parameters we need to adjust. The way this is done in practice will become clear in the following section, where the backpropagation algorithm is described.

# Understanding the backpropagation algorithm

There are two phases in the training process of a deep neural network: forward and back propagation. We have seen the forward phase in detail:

1. Calculate the weighted sum of the inputs:

$$wsumj = \sum_{i=1}^{N} w_{ji} . x_i$$

2. Apply the activation function to the result:

$$s_j = s(wsum_j) = \frac{1}{1 + e^{-wsum_j}}$$

Find different activation functions in the suggested reading at the end of the chapter. The sigmoid function is the most common and is easier to use, but not the only one.

3. Calculate the output by adding all the results from the last layer (N neurons):

$$Output = \theta_0 + \sum_{j=1}^{N} \theta_j \cdot s_j$$

After the forward phase, we calculate the error as the difference between the output and the known target value: *Error = (Output-y)².*

All weights are assigned random values at the beginning of the forward phase.

The output, and therefore the error, are functions of the weights $w_i$ and $\theta_j$. This means that we could go backward from the error and see how a small variation in each weight affects the result. This is expressed in mathematical terms as the derivative or gradient:

$$\frac{\partial Error}{\partial w_1}$$

This equation measures the change in the error every time we change $w_1$ by a small amount. We actually apply an activation function inside each neuron, so the change in error turns into the following equation (known as the chain rule):

$$\frac{\partial Error}{\partial w_1} = \frac{\partial Error}{\partial s} \cdot \frac{\partial s}{\partial w_1}$$

We want to change all weights values in the direction that decreases the error. This is the reason why the optimization method is called **gradient descent**. If we imagine the error as a function of two weights (there are more than two, of course, but we human beings have a hard time thinking beyond three dimensions!), we can picture this optimization as follows:

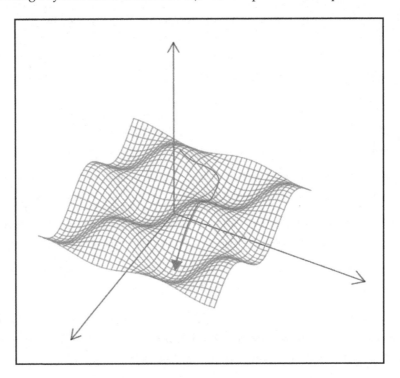

When are the weights adjusted? There are three methods:

- **Online**: With each new training sample, all weights are recalculated. This is very time-consuming and could lead to problems if the dataset has too many outliers.
- **Batch**: The weights are calculated for the whole training dataset, calculating the accumulated error and using it to correct them.
-  **Stochastic**: The batch mode is used taking small samples of the training data. This speeds up the whole process and makes the method more robust against local optimal values.

We are now familiar with how artificial neural networks are built and how their output is calculated. It is generally impractical to perform these calculations as the size of the network grows, as often happens for all practical and useful implementations.

# Summary

We have studied the basic principles of how artificial neural networks are built and how they learn from the input data. Even if the actual method, in practice, for using neural networks is different than what we have done in our example, our approach is useful in order to understand the details and to go beyond the idea that neural networks are mysterious black boxes that magically solve problems.

In the next chapter, we will see how we can use pre-built machine learning models available in Azure, connecting them to Excel to solve the problems we have presented up to now.

# Questions

1. Using the results of the perceptron test, build the confusion matrix and evaluate the quality of the prediction.
2. There is one important step that is missing in the binary classification problem that we solved with our artificial neural network, which might improve the result if we implement it. What did we miss? Hint: build an histogram of the binary variable that indicates whether there was a blood donation in March 2007.

# Further reading

- *Brief Introduction to Neural Networks* by David Kriesel, available online at http://www.dkriesel.com/_media/science/neuronalenetze-en-zeta2-1col-dkrieselcom.pdf
- *Neural Networks and Deep Learning* by Michael A. Nielsen, available online at http://neuralnetworksanddeeplearning.com/
- *Deep Learning: Using Algorithms to Make Machines Think,* https://opensourceforu.com/2017/12/deep-learning-using-algorithms-to-make-machines-think/

# 10
# Azure and Excel - Machine Learning in the Cloud

The clear tendency nowadays is to move all analysis, storage, and visualization activities to the cloud. In this chapter, you will find information about how to use Azure services and get a free subscription to test them. Deep learning seems to be the path to general Artificial Intelligence, that is, machines that can think as humans. We are not even close to that yet, but artificial neural networks are used in computer vision, text and speech analysis, and many other advanced applications. There are many use cases for artificial intelligence that are pre-built inside Azure and that can be used by building an experiment, as shown in detail in this chapter.

The following topics will be covered in this chapter:

- Introducing the Azure Cloud
- Using Azure Machine Learning Studio for free – a step-by-step guide
- Loading your data into Azure Machine Learning Studio
- Creating and running an experiment in Azure Machine Learning Studio

## Technical requirements

To complete this chapter, you will need a Microsoft account. If you don't have one, you can get one for free at https://signup.live.com/.

You will also need to download the titanic_small.csv file from the GitHub repository at https://github.com/PacktPublishing/Hands-On-Machine-Learning-with-Microsoft-Excel-2019/tree/master/Chapter10.

# Introducing the Azure Cloud

Cloud computing is the on demand availability of computer system resources, especially data storage and computing power, without direct active management by the user. The term is generally used to describe data centers available to many users over the Internet. Here are some advantages of using the cloud instead of on-premises computers:

- **Cost**: Instead of buying and maintaining expensive hardware and software, the cloud model offers to pay only for what is used.
- **Speed**: A large amount of resources can be obtained typically in minutes, just by configuring some settings in a website.
- **Global scale**: The size and location of the resources can be dynamically changed according to the user's needs.
- **Productivity**: IT staff can save time and focus on tasks that help the business grow, instead of doing hands-on maintenance of local equipment.
- **Performance**: The cloud servers are upgraded often and offer the latest available technology.
- **Security**: In spite of the usual worries related to storing and moving sensitive data to and from the cloud, most providers have adequate policies to protect the user's data.

The most important cloud providers, at the time of writing this book, are AWS, MS-Azure and GCP. We are going to focus on Azure and describe some of the services that are relevant for data analysis using machine learning.

Like all cloud providers, Microsoft includes all types of services in Azure. Our interest will be mainly in **Azure Machine Learning Studio (AMLS)**, which is designed to create and test machine learning projects and experiments easily.

# Using AMLS for free – a step-by-step guide

Microsoft AMLS is a tool that provides a drag and drop interface to build, test, and deploy machine learning models and analytics solutions. It is possible to publish models as web services that can be consumed from Excel (among other tools).

We will start by registering in the AMLS home page, using your Microsoft account:

1. Open `https://studio.azureml.net/`. You will see the following front page:

2. Click on **Sign up here** and you will get to the next page:

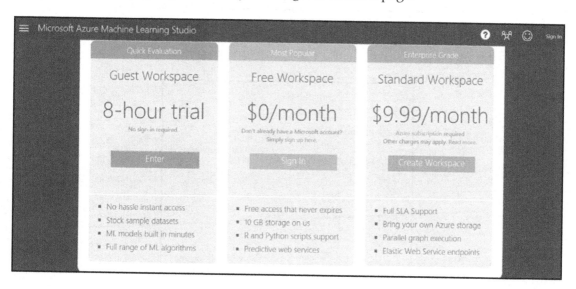

3. Choose the second option (that is, **Free Workspace**), which requires that you have a Microsoft account. The advantage is that this option is free and you can use it without limits. Once you click on the **Free Workspace** option, you will be taken to the following login screen:

4. Enter the username you chose when you created your Microsoft account and click on **Next**. You will then see the password input screen:

5. Type the password of your Microsoft account and click on **Sign in**.
6. You will be taken to the AMLS home page:

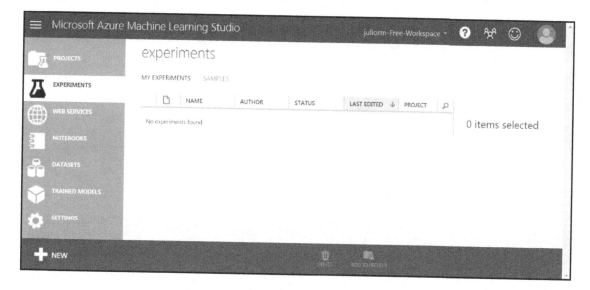

Now that you are ready to start, we will cover how to load your dataset into ALMS.

# Loading your data into AMLS

There is no machine learning project without data, so the first step in our analysis is to load the input file (titanic_small.csv) into AMLS. This is a simplified version of the Titanic dataset, which contains three features and one target variable:

- Features:
  - **pclass**: The class in which the passenger traveled (values 1, 2, or 3 corresponding to 1st, 2nd, and 3rd class)
  - **sex**: Passenger's gender (female or male)
  - **Age group**: Infant, child, teenager, adult, elderly, or unknown
- Target variable:
  - **Survived**: 1 if the passenger survived the shipwreck, 0 if they didn't.

To load the file, follow these steps:

1. From the home page, click on **DATASETS**. You will see an empty list of datasets:

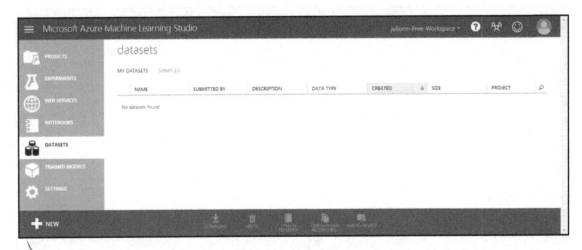

2. Click on **+NEW** to get a link to upload a local data file:

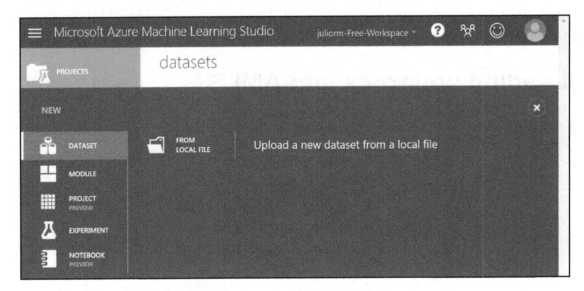

3. Click on **FROM LOCAL FILE** and you will see the following dialog box:

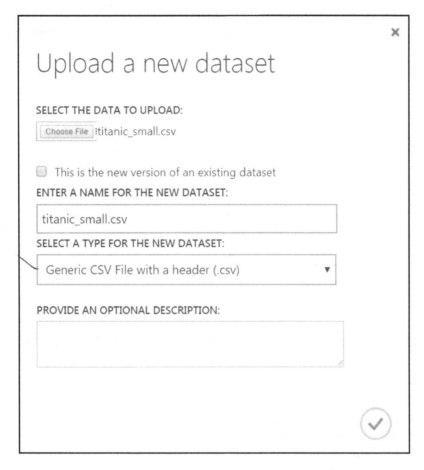

4. Click on **Choose File** and navigate to the input file (`titanic_small.csv`) location in your computer.
5. Enter any name you want for the dataset in the corresponding field.
6. Select the type of file, in this case **Generic CSV File with a header (.csv).**
7. Optionally, describe the contents of the data set for future reference.
8. Click **OK.**

9. You will see your recently uploaded dataset in the list:

You now have everything you need to start building your first experiment in AMLS. We'll do it together in the next section.

# Creating and running an experiment in AMLS

The basic components of AMLS are experiments. They are built by dragging and dropping predefined modules into a workspace. Each module has some defined task, a given number of parameters that can be chosen at runtime, and a defined number of input and output nodes. Here is a screenshot of the AMLS module:

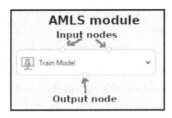

They can be connected to build an analysis workflow, from data input and transformation to machine learning model training and results. We will go step by step and create a machine learning experiment, training a decision tree to predict the survival of the Titanic passengers.

# Creating a new experiment

Perform the following steps to create a new environment:

1. From the home page, select **EXPERIMENTS**. You will see the empty list of experiments:

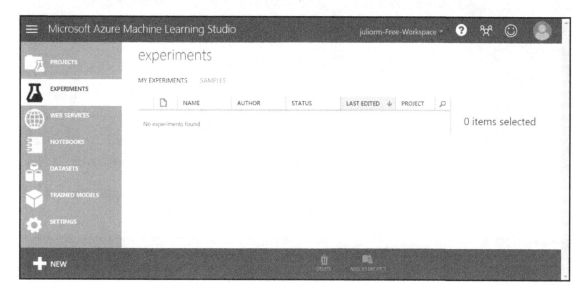

2. Click on **+NEW** to create a new Experiment. You will see the list of available experiments that can be loaded from the Azure catalog:

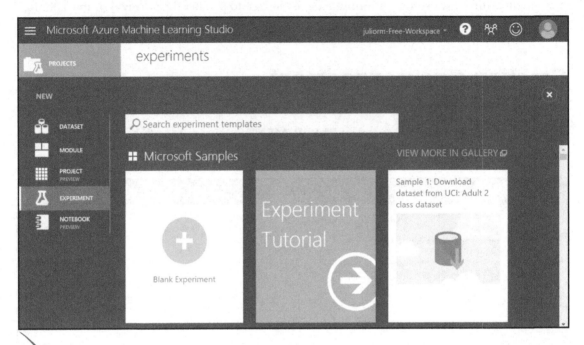

3. Click on **Blank Experiment** to create an empty one. The following screenshot shows how an experiment looks before you start to add modules:

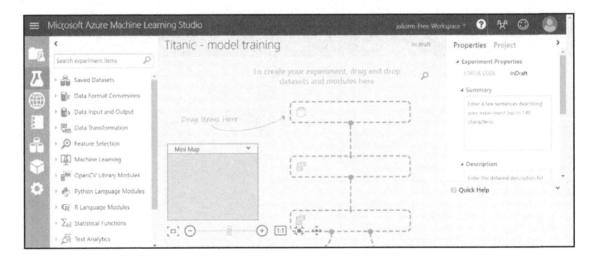

The left part is the module catalog, grouped by function. The middle (gray) area is the workspace, where we are going to drop the modules, and the right part shows a summary of the experiment. In the upper-left corner of the workspace, you can see the experiment name. You can click on it and edit the text. In our example, the text was edited to show **Titanic – model training**.

Once you are familiar with AMLS, explore the experiments in the catalog. They are good examples of the capabilities that AMLS can offer and the types of problems you can solve with it.

This first experiment will only use the input data to train the decision tree, and have it ready to use later in another experiment, which will be the one that predicts the survival of the passengers. We split the experiment into two parts because we want to train the tree only once and use it later for prediction. We will show a step-by-step guide to training the decision tree model in the next section.

# Training a decision tree model

1. In the module catalog, go to **Saved Datasets** | **My Datasets** and drag the "titanic_small.csv" into the right workspace module that contains our input data to the workspace. It contains the data previously read from the file. After dropping the data module, you should see something similar to the following screenshot:

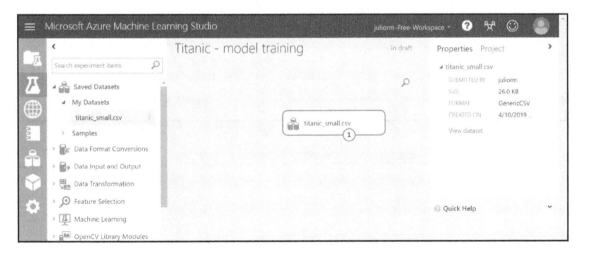

**TIP**

Clicking in a module after dropping it on the workspace will show information about it on the right-hand side of the screen.

2. Drag and drop two other modules, which represent the decision tree that we are going to train and a generic training module. The first one is located in **Machine Learning | Initialize Model | Classification | Two Class Boosted Decision Tree**. The second one is located in **Machine Learning | Train | Train Model**.

3. Once all modules are dropped into the workspace, you need to connect them to build a data flow. To connect two modules, do the following:

    1. Click on the output node of the first module.
    2. Keep the mouse button pressed and move the pointer to the input node of the second module.
    3. Release the mouse button. You should see a curved lines joining both modules.

4. The final set of connected modules should look like the following screenshot:

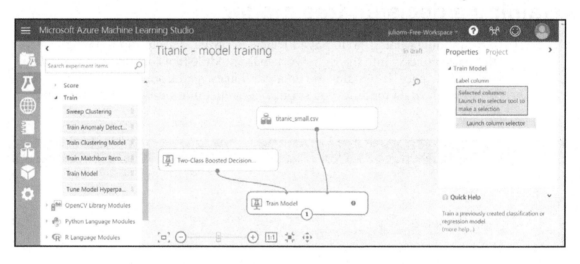

You need to select the target variable in the module labeled **Train Model**. To do that, perform these steps:

1. Click on the module.
2. Click on **Launch column selector** on the right-hand side panel.
3. In the pop-up window, click on **BY NAME**.
4. From the list of available columns, click on **survived**.
5. Click on the right arrow (>). This will move the **survived** variable to the right. You should see something similar to the following screenshot:

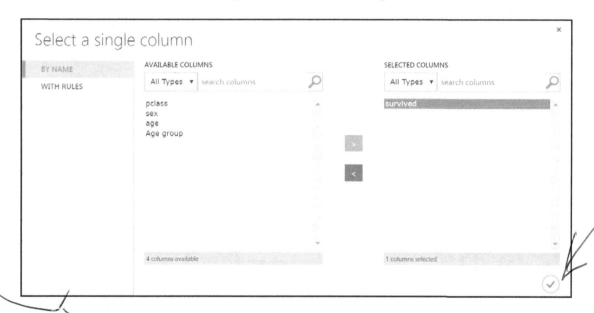

6. In the bottom menu, click on **RUN**:

7. Wait until the run finishes. It should only take a couple of minutes until you see a green tilde on all modules.

You can visualize the models that you trained. In this case, the default is to train 100 decision trees. To see them in detail, follow these steps:

1. Right-click on the **Train model** module.
2. Navigate to **Trained model | Visualize**:

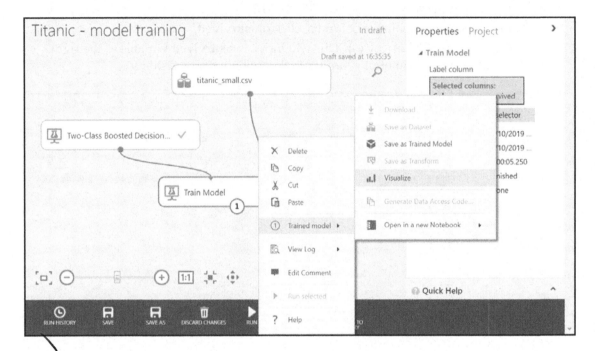

3. Choose any of the trees shown in miniature on the left-hand side to see the details. You can follow how decisions are made on each node of the tree and follow the branch values to the final value of the target variable. The following screenshot illustrates this:

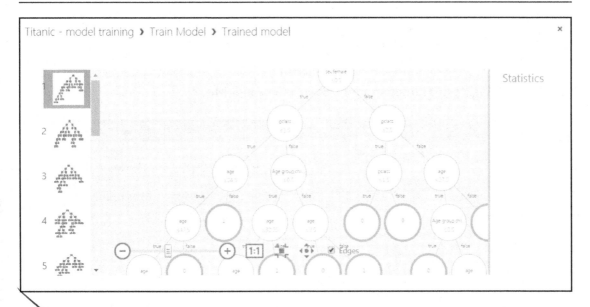

4. Clicking on the module labeled **Two-Class Boosted Decision Tree** shows a list of model parameters on the right-hand side panel. These parameters affect the training of a decision tree. You can change these parameters and run the experiment again:

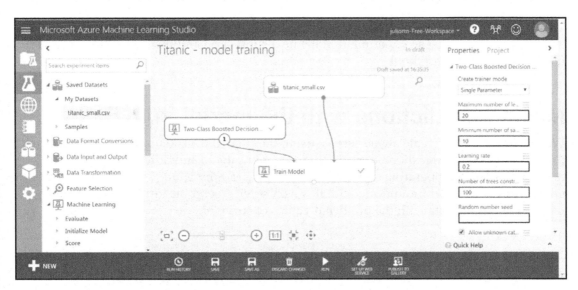

5. Save the experiment by clicking on **SAVE** in the bottom menu.

Finally, we are going to save the model for future use, whenever we want to predict the survival chance of a given passenger. To do so, follow these steps:

1. Right-click on the **Train model** module.
2. Navigate to **Trained model** | **Save as Trained Model**:

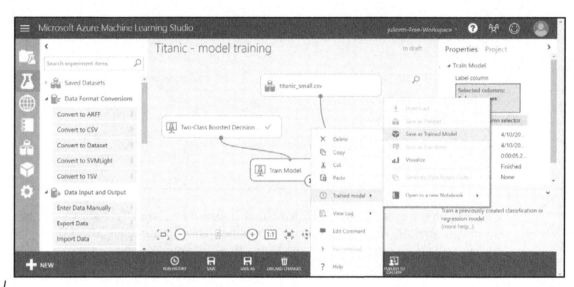

The model is now trained with the input dataset and ready to use in a new experiment. We are going to build such an experiment in the next subsection and then show how it can be used from an Excel workbook.

# Making predictions with the model from Excel

We are now going to create a web service using the trained decision tree. Web services are used to allow communication between different applications and different sources, and don't depend on the operating system or specific programming language. We are then going to use Excel to communicate with this web service, send the input data to it, and receive the output data with the predicted values of survival.

If you followed the instructions to create an experiment carefully, you should be now able to do it on your own, with some general guidance, as follows:

1. Create a new experiment and change its name to `Titanic - Web Service`.
2. Drag and drop five modules to the workspace:
   - **Saved Datasets** I **My Datasets** I `titanic_small.csv`: The dataset we loaded and used to train the decision tree.
   - **Trained Models** I **Titanic Model - Trained**: The trained model we saved for future use.
   - **Machine Learning** I **Score** I **Score Model**: That will be used to predict the target variable according to the model training.
   - **Web Service** I **Web Service Input** and **Web Service Output**: That will handle the communication of data from and to Excel.
3. Connect the modules so the experiment looks like the following screenshot:

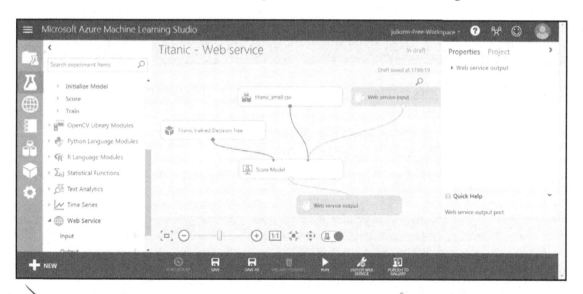

4. Save the experiment and run it.

The input data is not really used in the experiment, since the data for the prediction will eventually be sent from the application that uses the web service. In spite of this, the input data module needs to be included as a reference to the data format (names of the variables and total number of columns).

5. Once the run is successful, click on **DEPLOY WEB SERVICE** in the bottom menu. You will be taken to the following screen:

The web service is now created and AMLS lets you download an Excel file that is already connected to it.

6. Download the file from the link on the last row of the screen (**BATCH EXECUTION, Excel 2013 or later workbook**).

7. Open the Excel file on your computer. You should see a menu to the right of the workbook:

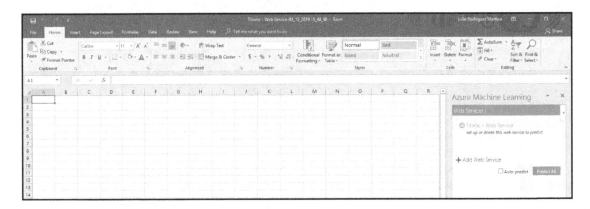

This means that the file is already connected to the web service we created.

8. Click on **Titanic – Web Service**. You will see the data input menu to the right:

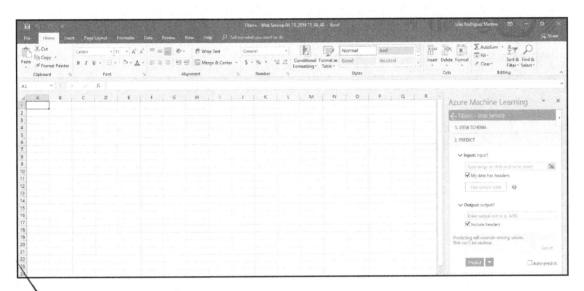

9. Click on **Use sample data** to get a few rows of data to use for predicting. You now have a table similar to the following:

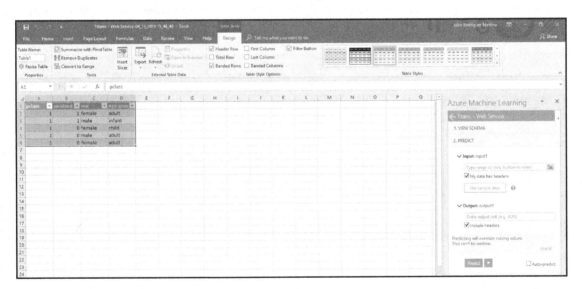

10. In the **Input** dialog box, write *A1:D6*.
11. In the **Output** dialog box, write the coordinates of the cell where you want the output data to start. In this example, we used *G1*:

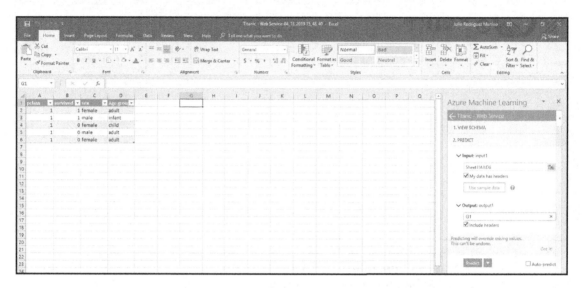

12. Click on **Predict**. The original table plus the predicted values will appear in the worksheet:

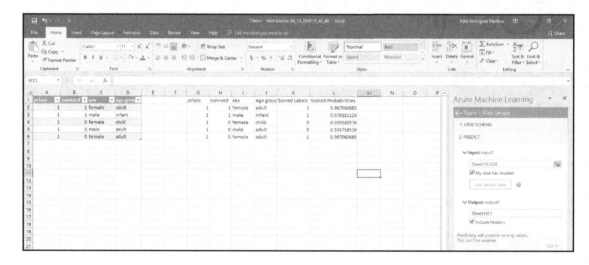

Data in the `survived` column is not taken into account for the prediction, since it is the target variable. It must be present to comply with the training data format.

Notice that four out of the five predicted values (in the `Scored Labels` column) agree with the values used for training. Predictions are never perfect and that is why it is so important to fine-tune the model parameters and carefully study the prediction error.

You now know how to build an experiment in AMLS and communicate with it from Excel, sending and receiving data. So, when you hear the phrase *cloud computing*, you know what it is about.

# Summary

We went through all the necessary steps to open an account in AMLS, a part of the Microsoft Azure cloud that helps us to build simple data and analysis flows. We also built two experiments: one of them trains a decision tree and the other predicts the target variable. Then we learned how to create a web service and connect Excel to it, sending and receiving data.

In the next chapter, we will show the present status of machine learning, which almost completely moves operations to the cloud, makes the data flows completely automatic, and uses automation to fine-tune the predictive models.

# Questions

1. What are the main advantages of using cloud computing?
2. Is cloud computing only useful for machine learning?
3. What is a web service and why is it useful?
4. If the model is already trained, why do we need to include the input data model in the analysis flow used for prediction?
5. Why did we split training and prediction into two different flows?

# Further reading

Check out the following resources for more information on the topics covered in this chapter:

- *Understanding the Basics of Cloud Computing*: `https://www.lucidchart.com/blog/cloud-computing-basics`
- *Azure Machine Learning Studio Documentation*: `https://docs.microsoft.com/en-us/azure/machine-learning/studio/`
- *Decision Trees Explained Easily*: `https://medium.com/@chiragsehra42/decision-trees-explained-easily-28f23241248`

# 11
# The Future of Machine Learning

Moving data analysis to the cloud is only one part of the way machine learning projects have changed over the last few years. Since the benefits of adding automation, **Artificial Intelligence (AI)**, and machine learning to many different parts of business operations are now clear and don't need further proof, companies are now focused on more permanent solutions. In fact, the natural follow-up is to think about finished products that can complete the full data cycle, from data collection to visualization.

There are many ways to create data analysis flows that can consume data as it is created and return results and visualizations after applying machine learning models. Cloud services make this task easier and more efficient.

Automatic machine learning is the current tendency in data analysis, where several machine learning models can be tested on the same dataset, automatically. Model parameters are optimized until the best model is found. This allows the concept of the *citizen data scientist*, its a role that analyzes data and creates data and business models for their companies with the help of big data tools and technologies. Citizen data scientists do not necessarily need to be data science or business intelligence experts. This role is given to employees in an organization who can use the big data tools and technology to create data models.

The following topics will be covered in this chapter:

- Automatic data analysis flows
- Re-training of machine learning models
- Automatic machine learning
- What can we expect in the future?

# Automatic data analysis flows

A few years before this book was written, businesses were approaching machine learning with the phrase *Let's see what this thing can do...* in mind. That is not the case any more. The value of using analytics, machine learning models, AI, and advanced visualizations to understand, simplify, and predict the outcome of many different situations is clear. This value is measured in terms of money, time, and effort savings, which leads to better and faster business decisions.

As a summary of what we have learned throughout this book, we can list the different parts of a data analysis flow:

- Data collection, usually from diverse sources
- Data cleansing and preparation, including exploratory visualizations
- Choosing a machine learning model that suits our data
- Training the model with historical data (if we are talking about supervised learning)
- Mining the data for hidden or unknown patterns (if we are talking about unsupervised learning)
- Testing the accuracy of the model prediction
- Fine-tuning the model parameters or changing the model if the results are not satisfactory
- Visualizing the results
- Periodically re-training the model with new data

The following schema illustrates these steps:

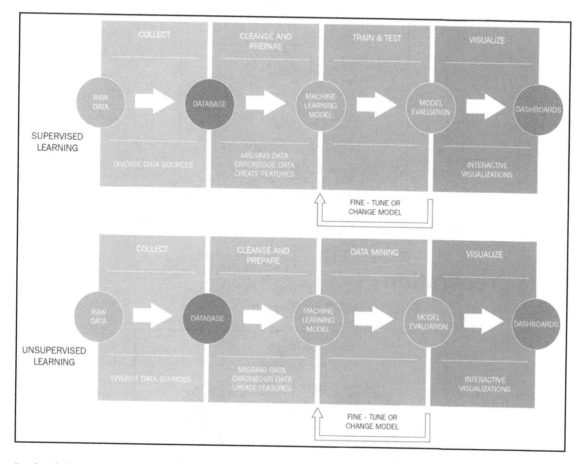

In the following subsections, we will discuss in detail how each of these steps is automatized.

# Data collection

Once the different data sources (on-premise files and databases) are identified, the data can be periodically uploaded to a cloud storage service. This is usually done automatically by a process running periodically, with minimal human intervention. There are many different storage options available from the main cloud service providers.

This concept is illustrated in the following diagram:

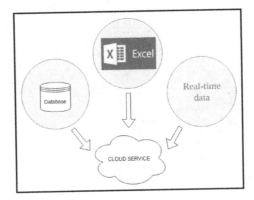

The next step is to prepare the data for feeding it into the models, that is, data preparation.

# Data preparation

The full data cycle is shown in the following diagram:

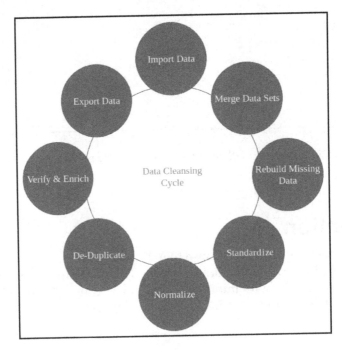

After importing data to the cloud service, the data cycle steps are as follows:

1. Merge datasets into a single table or set of connected tables. This might require some processing of the data to convert it to a suitable format.
2. Rebuild missing data, by replacing missing values or deciding to discard the incomplete entries.
3. Standardize the units of measure, decimal precision, and other characteristics of the data.
4. Normalize the data, especially if the machine learning model requires that.
5. De-duplicate, that is, remove redundant entries.
6. Verify the data quality using pre-defined criteria and enrich it by adding calculations.
7. Export the data to the next analysis phase, usually the machine learning models.

All cloud providers offer a built-in or third-party solution for data preparation. Some alternatives are Amazon QuickSight, the Azure Machine Learning Data Prep SDK, Cloud Dataprep in Google Cloud, and many others.

# Model training

The training cycle of a supervised machine learning model can be summarized as follows:

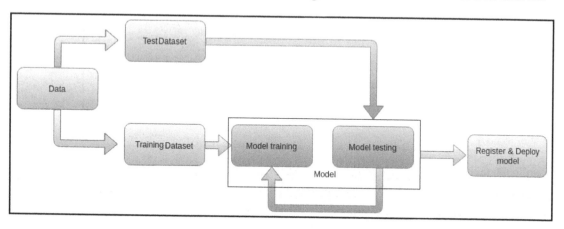

The prepared data is split into train and test sets. The test results give feedback to modify the model hyperparameters and the model type, and give hints as to the amount of data necessary to get good accuracy.

The final step is to deploy the model to make it available (for example, as a web service), but also to register everything that characterizes a particular training run. The type of model, all hyperparameters, and even the data used should be saved as metadata.

There are many pre-built models available for use in the cloud and methods to register and manage different models.

# Unsupervised learning

Whenever we are not sure of what we are going to find in data or we need to process a very large number of entries that would be impossible to manage manually, we use unsupervised machine learning. A general diagram could be as follows:

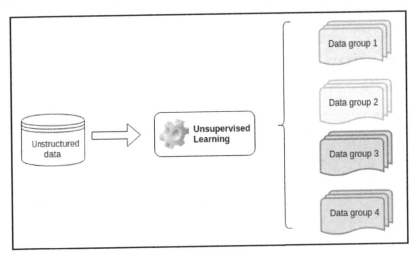

After going through the model, data is ordered and shows patterns that might be useful for making informed decisions. We can apply all of the models available in the cloud and then choose the one that better suits our needs for knowledge and understanding.

# Visualizations

The last step in the data flow is **visualization**. When presenting our results to a non-technical audience, stressing the benefits of our analysis is of paramount importance to show the value of what we do. Interactive dashboards are the usual way of doing this, with advanced tools such as **Tableau**, **Power BI**, or **QlikView**. Some examples can be found at the following URL: `https://www.clearpointstrategy.com/executive-dashboard-examples/`.

Every dashboard tool can be either used online or connected to the cloud to show the analysis results.

# Re-training of machine learning models

Since new data is available all the time and business conditions change, machine learning models need periodic re-training. Cloud services offer ways of doing this with minimum intervention, without the need to rebuild any part of the data flow. You only need to load new data and specify that you are not building a new model but re-training an existing one. After finishing, the model will be available for use as usual.

In this section, we have showed a full data analysis flow that can be completely hosted in the cloud. The section is also useful as a detailed summary of the book's contents. The next section outlines the real future of machine learning, when coding and manual work will be reduced to an absolute minimum.

# Automated machine learning

There are several tasks that are crucial for the success of a machine learning model when applied to solve a given business problem, for example:

- Data pre-processing
- Feature engineering
- Model selection
- Optimization of the model hyperparameters
- Analysis of the model results

These tasks were usually performed more or less manually by experts in the field. In recent years, there has been a growing interest in *democratizing* machine learning, allowing for non-experts (sometimes called *citizen data scientists*) to use, improve, and apply machine learning to concrete problems. **Automated Machine Learning (AutoML)** targets that specific need.

In general, the building process of a new model can be described as in the following diagram:

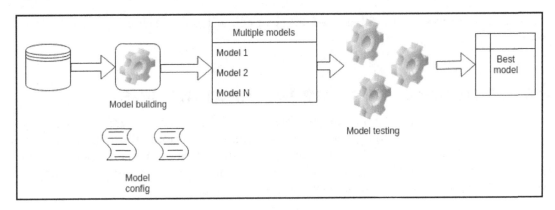

Following is the process for building of new model:

- Input data is pre-processed and used to build the best model features
- Based on some configurations done by the user, a given set of models is built and tested
- Models are evaluated and tested based on some criteria

Most of the work involved in developing, fine-tuning, and evaluating models is done automatically. The outcome is the best possible model, according to the input data and to the conditions given by the user.

Amazon, Google, and Microsoft all have AutoML capabilities, either using proprietary code or external packages. Alternative solutions exist, such as **TPOT** and **H2O.ai**.

The future of machine learning is already here. Without the need to write code and with minimum knowledge of a toolset, anyone can build a full data analysis flow. This is both an advantage and a risk: skilled analysts can test different options more quickly and optimize their work; unskilled people can use solutions such as black boxes without fully understanding how they work, possibly misunderstanding the results and making bad decisions. The ultimate responsibility belongs, as with any business tool, to the interested user.

# Summary

The last chapter of the book is thought of both as a summary of all chapters and as a window to what can be done beyond Excel and in the future. Automated data flows and machine learning model generation simplify analysts' work and speed up the decision-making process.

Hopefully, you now have a wide view of what machine learning is, how to use it in each line of business, and what are the most advanced alternatives to what was known before reading this book.

# Questions

1. What part of the analysis flow is different for supervised and unsupervised learning?
2. Why is data cleansing a continuous cycle?
3. Explain briefly what model hyperparameters are.
4. Which steps can be performed automatically by AutoML?

# Further reading

- *Azure Machine Learning Service Documentation*: https://docs.microsoft.com/en-us/azure/machine-learning/service/
- *Machine Learning on AWS*: https://aws.amazon.com/machine-learning/
- *AI and machine learning products*: https://cloud.google.com/products/ai/
- *Announcing automated ML capability in Azure Machine Learning*: https://azure.microsoft.com/en-us/blog/announcing-automated-ml-capability-in-azure-machine-learning/
- *H2O.ai*: https://www.h2o.ai/
- *Cloud AutoMLB*: https://cloud.google.com/automl/
- *AUTOML*: http://www.ml4aad.org/automl/

# Assessment

## Chapter 1, Implementing Machine Learning Algorithms

1. In classical programming, the code developed and run in the computer is a step-by-step set of instructions telling the computer what to do and how to handle different options. Machine learning is about showing the computer examples of data to either teach it what to do by example, or to let it learn information that is hidden in the data.

2. The machine learning models can be either regression (if the target variable is numerical and continuous) or classification (if the target variable is categorical or discrete).

3. Models that learn by example, training on labeled data, are called supervised machine learning models. In comparison, those that find information in the unlabeled data are called unsupervised machine learning models.

4. The following are the main steps that are needed when creating and using a machine learning model:
   1. Obtaining the data and merging different data sources
   2. Cleansing the data
   3. Preliminary analysis and feature engineering
   4. Trying different models and parameters for each of them, training them by using a percentage of the full dataset, and using the rest for testing
   5. Deploying the model so that it can be used in a continuous analysis flow and not only in small, isolated tests
   6. Predicting values for new input data

4. The $R_j$ residual is the difference between the $y$ value of the $j$ data point and the value of the regression line that is fit for that point:

$$R_j = (y_j - \hat{y}_j)$$

The **Mean Absolute Error (MAE)** is defined as follows:

$$MAE = \frac{1}{N} \sum_{j=1}^{N} |R_j|$$

The **Mean Squared Error (MSE)** is defined as follows:

$$MSE = \frac{1}{N} \sum_{j=1}^{N} (R_j)^2$$

4. Underfitting refers to a model that fails to represent the characteristics of the dataset. Even if this seems correct, it completely lacks generalization. Overfitting refers to a model that fits so well to the training data that it lacks generalization, and it would be wrong to test it against a different dataset.
5. They need to be encoded as binary variables first.

# Chapter 2, Hands-On Examples of Machine Learning Models

1. Encoding prepares categorical features in order to feed them into a machine learning model and does not assume any prior correlation between the encoded values.
2. By setting a limit to the length of the tree or by defining a minimum entropy value.
3. `Temperature_hot` is equally split; two values end in `Train_outside` = yes, and two values end in `Train_outside` = no. This represents the maximum entropy value, where there is no clear information about what to do if the temperature is hot.

4. The following IF statements would be considered when deciding whether or not to train outside:
   - If outlook is Sunny and it's not windy, then train outside.
   - If outlook is Sunny and it's windy, then don't train outside.
   - If outlook is Overcast, then Train outside.
   - If outlook is Rainy and Humidity is high, then don't train outside.
   - If outlook is Rainy and Humidity is normal, then train outside.

   It should be clear that this diagram is only an example and does not cover all the possibilities that can be derived from the data table.

5. The cluster distribution will depend on the initial choice of centroids. There are more advanced methods of building clusters in order to avoid this problem.
6. Visual clustering is based on two-dimensional diagrams, which only show the relationship between two variables. The numerical analysis takes into account all dimensions in the data.

# Chapter 3, Importing Data into Excel from Different Data Sources

1. Any character that is not confused with the file contents.
2. The outcome of a machine learning model will be affected by missing or incorrect data entries, and the correct format should also be used.
3. Importing an Excel file will open the Power Query interface in order to preprocess the data.
4. Data that is in a tabular form.
5. An exhaustive list can be found at https://gist.github.com/gelisam/13d04ac5a54b577b2492785c1084281f.
6. An example can be found at https://stackoverflow.com/questions/38120895/database-vs-file-system-storage.

# Chapter 4, Data Cleansing and Preliminary Data Analysis

1. Instead of building the decision tree manually, it would be interesting to study in-depth the example built-in Azure Machine Learning Studio, which was shown in Chapter 10, *Azure and Excel - Machine Learning in the Cloud*.
2. cabin and fare, pclass and fare, home.dest and fare are some examples.
3. Missing values could be replaced by the mean value of the variable.
4. Any unbalance in the dataset is referred to as bias. This will affect the results of any machine learning model, since the model will find more examples of a given class or some tendency to a particular target value.
5. You can, for example, try to see some correlations between variables using scatter plots.

# Chapter 5, Correlations and the Importance of Variables

1. You can, for example, build a diagram with the categorical values on the $x$ axis and the numerical values on the $y$ axis; any correlation would be clear from this diagram.
2. It should be easy for the reader to build diagrams and understand the relationship between variables.
3. No. It means that when a variable increases, the other variable decreases.
4. This formatting was used in Chapter 6, *Data Mining Models in Excel Hands-On Examples*.
5. We calculated the **Squared Error (SSE)** as *([@mpg]-[@prediction])^2*. The other sum we need is *SST = ([@mpg]-average([@prediction]))^2*. Then, we calculate $R^2 = 1-SSE/SST$.
6. You can try using an exponential function (*EXP()*) or another function with a similar shape. The $R^2$ value will probably still be far from 1, since the dispersion in the data is very high.

# Chapter 6, Data Mining Models in Excel Hands-On Examples

1. Use the previous knowledge of the business to discard these associations.
2. Not necessarily. These types of analysis are usually dependent on the business domain and even on the particular place where we perform them. This means that some results can be generalized, but, often, not all of them.
3. It means that there is no customer that started buying products by the time indicated in the column and that kept buying after the period of time shown in the row.
4. There are no customers that old (in terms of time spent as customers).
5. For example, focusing on those that stop buying and aiming ad campaigns at them.

# Chapter 7, Implementing Time Series

1. By setting `increasing(TravelDate)` to the moving average values in the calculation and following the same steps.
2. If the seasonality is too different from the real value in the data, then the prediction will have less accuracy. If we increase the confidence interval, then the error will also increase.
3. Using the `COVARIANCE.P` function in Excel.

4. The time series diagram, after applying the logarithm, will look like the following screenshot:

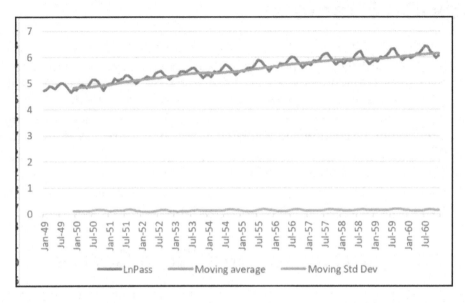

The trend is still ascending, but the standard deviation looks flat and is not dependent on the time.

# Chapter 8, Visualizing Data in Diagrams, Histograms, and Maps

1. It is very difficult to distinguish the different pie slices.
2. Multiple line charts.
3. You can get data from `https://openaddresses.io/` and follow the instructions in this article: `https://www.roguegeographer.com/create-your-own-maps-using-excel-3d-maps/`.
4. It is possible to do it and get a result, but the accuracy will be bad. The result of an election depends mostly on external factors that are not taken into account by the data, and not so much on the historical results of past elections.

# Chapter 9, Artificial Neural Networks

1. The result will depend on the artificial neural network training. You can follow the step-by-step instructions in the *Evaluating models* subsection in `Chapter 1`, *Implementing Machine Learning Algorithms*.
2. The dataset is unbalanced and that will affect the results.

# Chapter 10, Azure and Excel - Machine Learning in the Cloud

1. Cost, speed, global scale, productivity, performance, and security.
2. Cloud computing is useful for many different applications and, in fact, can replace everything that was built on-premise, from databases to visualizations.
3. Web services are applications hosted on the internet, which can communicate with other applications through predefined protocols and data formats. The advantage of using web services is that they are easy to share and are independent from the operating system and programming language used.
4. Azure Machine Learning Studio needs the input data format, and this is taken from the input data module.
5. The training flow is used to train the model and then save it. The same model is then used in a separate flow for prediction, without the need to retrain the model every time it is used.

# Chapter 11, The Future of Machine Learning

1. The model training and testing is replaced by data mining, which works by trying to get useful information from the data.

2. New data is included continuously into the data flow, and the full cycle must be fulfilled before feeding it into a machine learning model.

3. A hyperparameter value is set before starting the learning process and defines some characteristics of the model (for example, the number of cycles in an artificial neural network training model).

4. The following steps can be performed automatically by AutoML:
   - Data preprocessing
   - Feature engineering
   - Model selection
   - Optimization of the model hyperparameters
   - Analysis of the model results

# Index

## P

Pearson's coefficient of correlation
  calculating 112, 113
perceptron
  about 186, 187
  testing 194, 195
  training 188, 189, 190, 191, 192, 193
pie chart 166
Power BI 229
programming 10

## Q

QlikView 229

## R

Receiving Operating Characteristic (ROC) 24

## S

scatter diagram
  building 108, 109
Spearman's correlation 113, 115
stacked charts 165
supervised learning
  using, with decision trees algorithm 34
  using, with multiple linear regression 30, 32, 34

## T

Tableau 229

text file
  data, importing 60, 63, 65
time series
  about 143
  forecasting, automatically in Excel 152, 153, 154, 155
  implementing 143
  modeling 144, 145, 146, 147, 148, 149, 150, 151
  stationarity 155, 156
  values 155
  visualizing 144, 145, 146, 148, 149, 150, 151, 152
True Positive Rate (TPR) 23

## U

unbalanced datasets 102, 103, 104
underfitting
  versus overfitting 21
unsupervised learning
  with clustering 44, 45

## V

Visual Basic Applications (VBA) 127
visualization 229

## W

web page
  data, importing 70, 72

Made in the USA
Coppell, TX
03 January 2020

14022879R00142